STUDENT UNIT GUIDE

NEW EDITION

AQA A2 Sociology
Unit 4

Crime and Deviance

Tony Lawson

PHILIP ALLAN

Philip Allan Updates, an imprint of Hodder Education, an Hachette UK company, Market Place, Deddington, Oxfordshire OX15 0SE

Orders
Bookpoint Ltd, 130 Milton Park, Abingdon, Oxfordshire OX14 4SB
tel: 01235 827827
fax: 01235 400401
e-mail: education@bookpoint.co.uk
Lines are open 9.00 a.m.–5.00 p.m., Monday to Saturday, with a 24-hour message answering service.
You can also order through the Philip Allan Updates website: www.philipallan.co.uk

ISBN 978-1-4441-6281-3

First printed 2012
Impression number 5 4 3 2 1
Year 2016 2015 2014 2013 2012

Cover photo: Morganimation/Fotolia

Typeset by Integra, India

Printed in Dubai

Hachette UK's policy is to use papers that are natural, renewable and recyclable products and made from wood grown in sustainable forests. The logging and manufacturing processes are expected to conform to the environmental regulations of the country of origin.

P2035

Contents

Getting the most from this book

Examiner tips

Advice from the examiner on key points in the text to help you learn and recall unit content, avoid pitfalls, and polish your exam technique in order to boost your grade.

Knowledge check

Rapid-fire questions throughout the Content guidance section to check your understanding.

Knowledge check answers

1 Turn to the back of the book for the Knowledge check answers.

Summary

Summaries

- Each core topic is rounded off by a bullet-list summary for quick-check reference of what you need to know.

Questions & Answers

Exam-style questions

Examiner comments on the questions

Tips on what you need to do to gain full marks, indicated by the icon **e**.

Sample student answers

Practise the questions, then look at the student answers that follow each set of questions.

Examiner commentary on sample student answers

Find out how many marks each answer would be awarded in the exam and then read the examiner comments (preceded by the icon **e**) following each student answer. Annotations that link back to points made in the student answers show exactly how and where marks are gained or lost.

About this book

This unit guide is aimed at students taking the AQA A2 Sociology course. It covers the topic **Crime and Deviance**, which is examined within Unit 4 and is one of the two topics for assessment in the AQA examination. This topic is designed to give you a good understanding of the impact of crime and deviance to individuals and to society as a whole, as well as providing you with opportunities to demonstrate your understanding of the links between crime and deviance, theories, methods and other topics within sociology. In addition, there is a specific requirement to demonstrate your understanding of the links between sociological theory and methods and the study of crime and deviance. This is an important aspect of the 'stretch and challenge' that is an element of A-level specifications in all subjects.

How to use the guide

To get the best out of this guide, you need to use parts of it at different times throughout your course. From the beginning of your study of crime and deviance you should look at the **Content guidance** section. This provides you with an overview of what is included in the specification for crime and deviance. It is designed to make you aware of what you should know before the unit test. As you go through the crime and deviance topic, you should refer to the relevant section of the Content Guidance to check on your progress and ensure that you have made the appropriate connections to other parts of the course.

The **Question and Answer** section offers some mock exam questions on crime and deviance for you to try, together with some sample answers at A-grade and C-grade level. Examiner's comments are included on how marks are awarded at A2. To gain full advantage from this section, you should wait until towards the end of your entire A2 course. This is because the questions on crime and deviance, like all A2 questions, have a synoptic dimension, that is, they allow you to demonstrate your understanding of sociology as a whole and not just crime and deviance on its own. You should, therefore, make connections to sociological theories, to sociological methods and to other substantive topics that you have studied throughout your AS and A2 course, when they are appropriate. It makes sense, therefore, to attempt the practice questions and review the answers towards the end of your A2 course.

When you are ready to do this, look at the material provided and Example 1 question 01 and identify the specific areas of crime and deviance that the **item** and the **question** are concerned with. Then, identify the specific sociological theories and evidence that you can use to answer the question set. Having studied the question carefully, you should attempt to answer it, without looking first at the sample answer given. It is important that you attempt to answer the question without looking at the answer, so that you can use a comparison of your answer and the specimen answer to improve your performance. When you have completed your answer, study the A-grade student's answer and identify where you might have made other links. Look carefully at the examiner's comments to see where you might have been able to make other improvements. Do not neglect the importance of the different skills that you have to demonstrate. You should also look at the C-grade answer and, using the examiner's comments as a guide, rewrite your answer so that it would gain A-grade marks. You should then repeat the process for Example 1 question 02.

You should then try to answer Example 1 question 03, but there is an additional step to take for this question. Question 03 requires you to apply what you know and understand about research methods to a specific aspect or issue in crime and deviance. So, you need to 'audit' the question carefully to ensure that you know what area of crime and deviance is being asked about and which research method(s) you have to apply to it.

These activities are time-consuming and you should not attempt them in one go. Divide up the tasks you have to do into manageable chunks and complete the activities over a number of weeks. For example, you might want to focus on example 1 question 01 as a first task, then Example 1 question 02 at a later date, then Example 1 question 03 and so on for Example 2 questions 01, 02 and 03. Keep in mind that, as this will be happening towards the end of the course, you will need to have everything completed in good time for the examination. You will, therefore, need to know the date on which the Unit 4 exam is to be held. You should then be able to fit these activities around your other revision tasks. In addition to using the questions to develop your examination skills, you could also use the answers as a source of revision material. Just reading through the A-grade student's answers should provide you with useful reminders of important sociological material.

The A2 specification

The aims of the A2 Sociology course are to enable you to:
- acquire knowledge and a critical understanding of contemporary social processes and social changes, and an understanding of the important part that social structure and social action play in them
- appreciate the significance of theoretical and conceptual issues in sociological debate
- understand and evaluate sociological methodology and a range of research methods
- develop a sustained interest in social issues
- develop skills that enhance your ability to participate more effectively in society
- allow you to develop critical and reflective attitudes that encompass a respect for social diversity and an awareness that others may have different interpretations of social experiences

Content guidance

About this section

This section is intended to show you the major issues and themes covered in **Crime and Deviance** and the main links that can be made to other areas of the course, to sociological methods and to sociological theories. You must remember, though, that these are offered as guidance only. The points included are not exhaustive (that is, other perfectly legitimate points may be raised by you). You will find many other concepts and studies relevant to your exploration of crime and deviance.

The content of Crime and Deviance falls into five main areas:
- theories of crime and deviance
- the social distribution of crime and deviance and recent trends in crime
- globalisation, the media and crime, green crime, human rights and state crimes
- crime control, victims and the criminal justice system
- the sociological study of suicide

In addition, throughout these content areas, you must be aware of the connections between sociological theory and methods and the study of crime and deviance.

The AQA A2 topic of Crime and Deviance is designed to give you a comprehensive understanding of the major sociological explanations of crime and deviance in contemporary societies.

The social distribution of crime and deviance is another important area of study and this covers distribution according to the social characteristics of age, social class, ethnicity, gender and locality. It also necessitates looking at how statistics of crime are constructed.

There are a number of issues included in the Content Guidance that have come to the forefront of the sociological study of crime and deviance. These can be seen loosely as 'contemporary concerns'. This includes the relationship between the media and crime, globalisation, environmental (or green crime) and the whole area of human rights violations and state crimes.

You will also need to be aware of the role and activities of the criminal justice system and its agents in the police and courts, as well as issues to do with punishment and the victims of crime.

The issue of suicide has always been one of great interest to sociologists, as it seems to be the most individual of acts and you will have to explore the sociological aspects of suicide.

When you have covered all these areas, you will have completed the topic (and the course). During your study of crime and deviance and as part of your synoptic understanding, you will need to identify when the two core themes of **culture, identity and socialisation** and **stratification, power and differentiation** are being addressed.

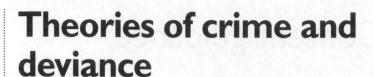

Theories of crime and deviance

Sociocultural tradition (Chicago School, strain and subculture theory)

Key ideas

Chicago School

- Patterns of crime in cities are not random.
- Highest levels of crime found in areas of highest social disorganisation.
- These would be located in the 'zone of transition', where there are high rates of migration and divorce, poor housing and communal facilities, family instability and unemployment.
- Such areas retain high levels of disorder, even though the population may change through internal migration.
- Social control of delinquents is easier where there are dense communal networks, and therefore high levels of 'incivility' (a lack of interest in the locality) are associated with high rates of offending.
- Contact with different levels of favourable and unfavourable attitudes to the law and the police in particular urban areas will lead to differential crime rates.
- 'Collective efficacy', where community members are prepared to act against low-level crime themselves reduces the incidence of more major crime in a locality.

Strain theory

- In mainstream society, there are agreed goals towards which individuals are taught to strive, and legitimate means of achieving them.
- Where there is 'strain' between goals and means, **deviant activity** emerges.
- Deviant and criminal activity can take several forms, depending on the nature of the strain, ranging from retreatism (for example, dropping out) to innovation (for example, thieving).
- Strain may be experienced not only in economic life, but also in personal life, such as the loss of a loved one.
- 'Social bulimia', where lower class individuals are **included** in society's desire to be materially well-off, but **excluded** from the means of achieving that wealth, is a feature of late modern societies.
- Where a society is 'strained' to the point of collapse 'failed societies' emerge that are havens for lawlessness and terrorism.

Subculture theory

- Those who are non-achievers in mainstream society develop an alternative **subculture** based on hedonism and machismo.

Knowledge check 1

What do sociologists call the contact between favourable and unfavourable attitudes towards the law?

Deviant activity
Behaviour that may be legal or illegal, but which is disapproved of in society (by someone or some institution).

Subculture An identifiable minority group in society who are organised around common values and/or patterns of behaviour that are distinct from mainstream society.

- Delinquent subcultures are linked to illegitimate opportunity structures, present in the zone of transition.
- Alternative subcultures exist in the inner city, from the retreatist subculture of the drug-taker to the conflict subculture of the gang.
- The lower class has focal concerns that emphasise masculinity and excitement, which lead members into risk-taking and non-conforming behaviour.
- Socialisation into narrow family and peer networks brings individuals into conflict with the wider society, but contact with these wider networks, such as school or community, decreases the incidence of delinquent behaviour.
- Subcultures of violence emerge where the 'code of the street' insists that respect from peers is the lynchpin of status in circumstances of deprivation and any 'disrespect' is met with a strong response.

Socialisation The process whereby individuals learn the norms and values of the society (or subculture) in which they live.

Evaluation

+ Chicago School established the city — especially inner city — as a focal point for research into crime and disorder.

+ The concept of social disorganisation is statistically linked with areas of high official crime rates.

+ Strain theory established a societal context for the study of crime and deviance.

+ Strain theory suggests a variety of responses to situations of frustration, not just criminal activity.

+ Strain theory can be applied at the macro (societal) level as well as the micro level.

+ Subcultural theory established the importance of group norms and values as generators of pro- and anti-crime attitudes.

+ Subcultural theory offers an account of deviance/crime that is located within the participants' own terms of reference and understanding.

− Chicago School assumes a degree of homogeneity in inner-city communities that is not always easy to show.

− Chicago School takes the official statistics of offending as the 'true' picture of crime, when much crime in other areas of the city goes undetected.

− Strain theory assumes that there is a general consensus about legitimate goals in society.

− Strain theory does not spell out why any one individual becomes a retreatist rather than a rebel, for example.

− Strain theory over-simplifies the processes that lead to a 'failed state'.

− Subcultural theory focuses exclusively on delinquent boys and ignores phenomena such as female gangs.

− It has been difficult to show empirically the existence of distinctive subcultures within inner-city areas.

− All these theories tend to assume that most crime is committed by the lower classes and ignore white-collar and other types of crimes of the powerful.

Examiner tip

Practise doing examination questions regularly and not just as you approach the examination. Familiarity improves performance.

Synoptic links

To methodological issues

The Chicago School established a methodological tradition based on the collection of empirical data, combined with 'appreciative sociology' that allowed those investigated to tell their own stories. This was an early combination of quantitative and qualitative measures. In looking at the 'geography' of crime, the Chicago School used statistics that indicated the distribution of crime in different urban areas. Strain theory is more interested in the social reaction of people to situations of strain and therefore a questionnaire or an interview might be a useful research tool to explore the individual's responses to strain. Subcultural theories are interested in how subcultures form and operate and thus might be open to more observational methods.

To other areas of the course

The Chicago School was interested in the 'passing on' of pro- and anti-crime attitudes through socialisation in the family — the 'primary level' of socialisation. These theories focused on the inner-city working-class male as the main perpetrator of crime, which has implications for policing in a class-stratified society.

To theoretical issues

Though a relatively 'old' theory of crime, the Chicago School influence can be seen in the growth of 'environmental criminology', which advocates 'target-hardening' strategies to make it more difficult for crimes to be committed. The followers of the Chicago School, strain theory and subculture theory tended, therefore, to adopt a positivistic approach to the study of crime and deviance.

Key concepts

zone of transition, social disorganisation, incivility, differential association, strain, conformity, retreatism, innovation, rebellion, ritualism, status frustration, focal concerns, network analysis, social bulimia

Key thinkers

Park and Burgess, Shaw and McKay, Sampson and Groves, Sutherland, Merton, Cloward and Ohlin, Miller, Bartol and Bartol, Young

Control theory

Key ideas

- Basic human nature is one of selfishness, with the result that everyone would commit crime if they could get away with it, in order to satisfy their needs.
- Therefore, crime results when the individual lacks self-control or where there are insufficient social controls to ensure conformity from individuals.
- Inner containment to prevent criminal actions includes attachment to family, strong orientation towards legitimate goals and psychological predispositions.
- Outer containment includes attachment to community, strong identity with peers and reinforcement of identity by others.
- The social bonds that an individual has (or does not have) are central in explaining conformity (or criminality).
- As individuals grow older, the social bonds they have intensify (having a family of their own for example) and so commitment to criminality weakens.
- Criminals lack self-control in many areas of social life, such as in smoking or drug taking, and their decision to commit a crime results from both poor self-control and the presentation of an opportunity to engage in a crime, with minimal risk.
- Society can reduce criminal activity by making it more difficult for opportunist criminals to target their victims.
- Life-course theorists argue that they were life-course persistent and adolescent-limited delinquents, with the delinquents suffering from a 'maturity gap', so that as they gained the right to adult activities, they became less criminal.

Social controls The ways in which society seeks to discipline individuals to create an orderly social environment.

Knowledge check 2

What do criminologists call actions that make it more difficult for criminals to commit crime?

Evaluation

+ Looks at the pressures to conform in society and the social control arrangements needed to reduce levels of crime.

+ Insists that individuals are making choices when they commit deviant or criminal acts and are not 'forced' to do them.

+ Target-hardening policies are popular with those who live in areas of high crime.

+ Looks at long-term engagement with the young and their desistance from crime.

− Assumes that everybody would commit crime if given the chance to do so without detection, but this cannot be shown to be the case.

− Over-emphasises the commitment of individuals to deviant activity, which is, more often than not, a transitory, episodic action.

− Seems to suggest that members of the middle class have more self-control than the working class.

− Control theorists are split between those who emphasise the continuity of criminality into adulthood and those who see desistance as the main trajectory.

Examiner tip
Try to read a quality newspaper every day or, failing that, at least a quality Sunday newspaper.

Operationalise To take an abstract concept, such as social class, and develop questions or attitudinal scales that can be used in a practical way in questionnaires and interviews etc.

Synoptic links

To methodological issues

Much control theory relies on self-report studies and there are doubts about the validity of the findings of these. Some of the factors in the concept of inner containment are difficult to operationalise and explore. Life-course theorists adopt a longitudinal approach to the study of delinquency, because they are interested in the persistence in or desistance of criminal behaviour throughout individual lives.

To other areas of the course

The focus of self-control is on the family and the socialisation process. Control theorists see the lack of a stable home environment and the absence of a strong moral upbringing as resulting in weak inner containment. Parents who do not establish clear lines of child behaviour are responsible for later delinquency.

To theoretical issues

Control theory is often linked to Durkheimian and functionalist sociology, because they share a pessimistic view of human nature. They see men and women as basically out for their individual selves, and therefore in need of strong social pressures to keep them law-abiding.

Key concepts

techniques of neutralisation, inner containment, outer containment, social bonds, power-control theory, self-control theory, administrative criminology, life course theory

Key thinkers

Reckless, Hirschi, Hagan, Gottfriedson and Hirschi, Coleman, Moffit, Sampson and Laub

Interactionist theories

Key ideas

- The activities of the law and the social control agencies such as the police and the courts are central in shaping the pattern of crime and deviance in society.
- Everyone breaks the law, but only certain individuals and groups are targeted by the police and courts to be labelled as criminal or deviant.
- Society reacts differently to those who have been labelled in this way from the rest of the population.

- Once labelled, the criminal or deviant begins to act in ways that confirm the label.
- Choices made by the police over where to patrol, whom to stop and search, whom to arrest and whom to move to prosecution, are important aspects of the operation of micro-power and shape the pattern of apparent criminal activity that emerges.
- Those labelled criminals are not inevitably cast out from mainstream society. In areas of strong communities, shame can be used to reintegrate the offending individual into society.
- Phenomenologists emphasise the meaning of crime for the individuals who commit crimes, focusing on the sense of excitement that they report while engaging in illegal activity.
- The labelling of groups as deviant or criminal can serve political purposes. By keeping the population fearful of crime or 'others', stronger laws can be introduced to curtail civil liberties.

Evaluation

+ Focuses attention on the role of the agents of social control in the 'production' of deviance.

+ Establishes the relative nature of the definition of crime and deviance.

+ Sees official statistics as socially constructed.

+ Phenomenological approaches show the importance of not just relying on 'official' accounts of deviant/criminal behaviour.

− Tends to trivialise serious deviant/criminal activity such as murder or rape.

− Minimises importance of the initial deviant/criminal act.

  Not all labelling is counter-productive — it can act to have an opposite effect.

− Ignores structural and ideological processes that shape the responses of society and the social control agencies to particular activities.

Synoptic links

To methodological issues

- Labelling is not easy to investigate empirically, as it is difficult to establish the importance of factors that lead to an individual's self-image. It is also difficult to identify primary deviants because, by definition, those who come to the sociologist's attention as 'criminal' have to be secondary deviants.
- Participant observation is the interactionist's preferred method and this has many difficulties, not least of which is whether two observers would interpret the same events in different ways. The nature of many deviant and/or delinquent groups makes it difficult for some sociologists to study them through observation. For example, it would be unlikely that an older sociologist would be accepted by a teenage gang as a member of their group.

Knowledge check 3

What do sociologists call it when someone labelled begins to act in ways that confirm the crime?

Micro-power The day-to-day, mundane exercise of power in our lives, in contrast to force, war, violence, prison etc.

Examiner tip

Practise applying your sociological skills to contemporary news events, asking yourself how sociologists would approach the issue.

Participant observation The sociologist takes part in the activities of the group under study either with the agreement of the group or as a hidden observer.

To other areas of the course

Labelling is also an important process in the education system, suggesting that those labelled as successes or failures tend to conform to their teachers' expectations of attainment, depending upon the label attached.

To theoretical issues

The interactionist approach adopted by labelling theorists leads to a lack of consideration of structural issues that might influence the distribution of deviance. Interactionists would argue against the existence of structures in society, focusing only on the meanings and intentions of individuals themselves. Structuralists argue that this is to neglect some deeper process at work in society that is important in explaining the existence and distribution of crime/deviance.

Key concepts

labelling, primary deviance, secondary deviance, self-fulfilling prophecy, master status, ecological bias, reintegrative shaming, cultivation thesis

Key thinkers

Becker, Lemert, Sampson, Braithwaite, Katz, Gerbner

Conflict theories

Key ideas

- The poor commit crimes as part of the struggle to live in an unfair capitalist society that dominates their lives, while the rich commit crimes to further their interests in a capitalist society that demands they acquire as much wealth as possible, under the ethic of individualism.
- Capitalism is crimogenic — the ultimate cause of all criminal activity in society.
- Capitalism generates a surplus population who are of no economic use to the system and who turn to crime in response to their situation of being outcasts.
- Left-wing idealists see criminals as the victims of capitalism — in order to survive they are forced into activity defined as illegal by those who hold power in society.
- Laws under capitalism are created in favour of the dominant social forces and are administered with a bias against subordinate groups in society.
- Criminal law is the product of an alliance between corporate business and the state.
- Governance has moved to a new punitiveness as the ruling class reacts strongly to challenges to its legitimacy.

Knowledge check 4

Give two examples of subordinate groups in society.

- All deviance and crime has a political dimension and crime waves are often used as a distracting device to focus the population's attention away from capitalism's economic crises.
- Deviant youth subcultures are a way for working-class youth to rebel against the system through adopting styles disapproved of by mainstream society.

Crime wave An intensification of a particular type of criminal activity, such as burglary.

Evaluation

+ Highlights the macro influences on crime and deviance, both ideological and economic.

+ Has a focus on law making as well as law breaking.

+ Examines the way in which the choices of social control agencies are influenced by dominant ideologies of who constitutes the criminal.

− Ignores the role of law in protecting all members of society, not just the powerful.

− Socialist societies also have high levels of crime.

− Left-wing idealism tends to romanticise the deviant and criminal at the expense of the victim.

Examiner tip
Identify real-life contemporary examples of a sociological concept to use in your examination. For example, the British government's response to the urban riots of 2011 could be argued to be an example of new punitiveness.

Synoptic links

To methodological issues

The use of content analysis of both media products and semiotic interpretation of 'styles' by conflict theorists has been an important contribution to an understanding of the role of the media in promoting images and ideologies associated with deviant and criminal subcultures. The objects of such investigations (newspaper articles, television programmes etc.) are conducive to investigation by content analysis, but have the disadvantage of being subjective interpretations.

To other areas of the course

The issues of economic power and control are important in a number of other areas, not just crime and deviance. In particular, the way that social class is created and reproduced under capitalism and the subordinate position of the working class are important in understanding the apparent concentration of crime in the lower classes. The unequal distribution of wealth and income are also seen in the Marxist analysis of crime and deviance as significant factors in the generation of material crimes.

Economic power The many ways in which controlling resources in society can give one the ability to affect and control one's own and other people's lives.

To theoretical issues

The role of crime and deviance in supporting or undermining capitalist societies is an issue much discussed in the Marxist approach to crime. For example, Marxists see homosexuality as stigmatised because it represents a 'threat' to the reproduction of the next generation of workers who are needed for the survival of capitalism.

Key concepts

crimogenic, economic determination, selective law enforcement, resistance through rituals, bricolage, new punitiveness

Key thinkers

Quinney, Chambliss, Taylor, Hall, Centre for Contemporary Cultural Studies, Beckett and Sasson

Left realist theory

Key ideas

- The study of crime must be true to the reality of crime and thus focus on the activities of working-class criminals in relation to their mainly working-class victims.
- The focus of investigation in the sociology of crime must be on four 'players': the activities of the police, the public, the criminal and the victim.
- Crime is concentrated among the lower class because members of this group are more likely to be marginalised from society and subject to relative deprivation.
- Marginalisation and relative deprivation vary over time and so crime rates will also vary.
- As the routines of individuals and groups change, so will their potential exposure to the risk of crime, so that more women going out to work increases female chances of becoming victims.
- Relative deprivation, rather than absolute poverty, is an important motivator towards crime, as people feel resentment towards those more wealthy than they are and do not have the possibilities to better themselves.
- Working-class subcultures, especially those that emphasise masculinity and risk-taking, are also, in the broadest sense, factors in the motivation to crime.
- These factors do not just lead to economic crime, but to other forms of criminality and deviance, such as drug-taking, wife-beating etc.
- The task of left-inclined sociologists is to offer practical programmes to the victims of crime, mainly in the working class, and in the form of self-help and community-based programmes.

Evaluation

+ Focuses attention on the working-class victims of much working-class criminal activity.

+ Insists that the 'fear of crime' is an important aspect of social living.

Knowledge check 5

What do sociologists call the interaction between these four players?

Marginalisation The process whereby some social groups are pushed towards the edges of mainstream society and excluded from many of its activities.

Examiner tip

Use your school or local library to widen your reading around issues — the more sophisticated your understanding, the higher your marks will be.

+ Reestablishes issues of policing as an important dimension of the sociology of crime and deviance.

+ Offers an economic context for crime.

− Does not explore non-working-class crime in any serious way.

− Assumes that it is easy to identify criminals and non-criminals in working-class communities.

− Tends to dismiss female criminality.

− Is idealistic about working-class communities controlling their own criminal element.

Synoptic links

To methodological issues

Many left realist studies are based on small-scale victim surveys carried out in the inner city. Some critics argue that though they listen carefully to the 'voices' of the victims of crime, they overlay these with their own interpretation of what is going on, without reference to the victims' points of view. This is an interesting methodological point, in that questionnaires and interviews may be the best way of allowing victims to have a voice, but they are still filtered through the mediation of the sociologist.

To other areas of the course

Because of the focus on the economic factors of marginalisation and relative deprivation, links can be made to the topic of wealth, poverty and welfare

To theoretical issues

While the left realists reject the more idealistic views of right idealists and the more condemnatory views of the New Right, they are still optimistic about the chances of controlling crime through the political activity of the working class. This can be criticised as a naive view, which tends to see the working class through rose-tinted glasses.

Mediation A person or a process stands between two phenomena and acts to interpret, explain or represent what is going on.

Key concepts

the square of crime, the fear of crime, routine activities theory, marginalisation, relative deprivation, subcultures of masculinity

Key thinkers

Young, Matthews, Lea, Cohen and Felson, Currie

Right realist theory

Key ideas

Consensus General agreement.

- There is a consensus in society that people and property should be protected against wrong doing.
- The state has an obligation to deter criminality and punish offenders.
- Traditional values, such as the belief in a strong nuclear family, help to prevent criminal behaviour.
- Individuals have biological predispositions to risk taking and therefore to criminality.
- Individuals make the choice to commit or not to commit crime, based on their predispositions and a calculation of the rewards and penalties that might arise from committing a crime.

Knowledge check 6

What do you understand by the underclass?

- Those most likely to give in to their biological dispositions to crime are to be found in the underclass, where traditional family forms and therefore socialisation into moral codes are weakest.
- The welfare state has weakened the interest of members of the underclass in legitimate employment, and they have therefore turned to illegal activity as a source of income.
- Crime prevention should focus on the opportunities to commit crime, making the effort to commit crime much harder and the penalties associated with it much stiffer.
- Small changes in the environment can tip the balance towards law-abiding behaviour, by making the consequences of criminality less attractive; for example, 'sleeping policemen' harming a car's suspension.

Evaluation

+ Accords with common-sense thinking about the leniency of the courts towards criminals.

+ Situates criminal actions within the choices that individuals make to commit or not to commit crime.

+ Critical of explanations of criminality that excuse criminal behaviour.

+ Offers clear advice on the direction of criminal justice policy.

− It is not always obvious what traditional values are.

− Is a populist rather than a sociological approach.

− Based on crude biological determinism.

− Ignores socioeconomic influences on crime and deviance.

Examiner tip

Develop a consistent way of taking notes, as your notes provide a solid base for revising for the examination.

Synoptic links

To methodological issues

The concepts that the New Right employ in relation to their investigations have often been criticised as vague and difficult to operate. For example, the 'approval of peers', used in considerations of **macho** underclass culture is hard to explore empirically. Rather, the concepts are attacked as constructs, used to justify a particular ideological position. One research method that has been used to test the claims of the right realists is that of using local crime statistics — for example, comparing rates of offending before and after the installation of CCTV in an area. This is a classic 'field experiment' and well suited to an investigation of whether CCTV reduces crime or not.

Macho Short-hand for machismo; a stereotyped version of what it means to be male, in which pride, toughness and dominance are key elements.

To other areas of the course

The focus of the New Right on the family is central to understanding their explanations of crime and deviance. It is a particular form of the family (lone parent headed by a single mother) that is seen by the New Right as the defining characteristic of an underclass whose members habitually engage in criminal or deviant behaviour.

To theoretical issues

The ideas of the New Right have provoked much controversy among sociologists. Some see them as a necessary counter-balance to the idealism of conflict theories, while others argue that they represent a political position that uses victims as scapegoats for phenomena of which they morally disapprove.

Key concepts

re-moralisation, constitutional factors, situational criminology, rational choice theory, underclass, welfare dependency, involvement decisions, event decisions

Key thinkers

Marsland, Wilson and Herrnstein, Cornish and Clarke, James Q. Wilson, Murray

Postmodern theory

Key ideas

- The underclass in postmodern societies has been cut off from mainstream society as unemployment and the decline of the welfare state have reduced its members' reasons for commitment to society.

Discourse of progress A particular 'story' or account of history that presents the flow of events over time as one of continual improvement.

Knowledge check 7

What is meant by discourses in sociology?

Self-surveillance Individuals act to police their own behaviour, assuming that all their actions are being monitored all of the time.

- As the mainstream society rejects the 'discourse of progress' and leaves the underclass to its own devices, the underclass loses all stake in obeying the law.
- In postmodern societies, the inability of many to satisfy their material needs in a society dominated by consumerism leads to an 'intensification of resentment' against those who can.
- Crime for individuals becomes a possibility when they feel they do not have any ties of obligation to the people they are targeting.
- Discourses that deny others their humanity are important in creating a climate in which actions that might harm those individuals are made acceptable.
- Social control in postmodern societies is achieved through seduction (being attracted by the consumerism of postmodernity) or repression (of those who do not share in the consumer society).
- The rise of new technologies has made the surveillance and control of the population easier, as individuals practise a form of self-surveillance.
- Postmodern societies are characterised by the extension of the micro-techniques of surveillance into our everyday lives through the routine activities of bureaucracies such as schools.

Evaluation

+ Focuses attention on informal justice within localities.

+ Emphasises that state power is everywhere all the time for everyone, not just in response to criminal activity by wrong doers.

+ Sees language/discourse as the main way that societies shape what can and cannot be done.

+ Can explain contemporary developments such as dope testing, consumer tracking, speed cameras etc.

− Postmodernist developments have not been empirically tested, in the main.

− Its relativism undermines notions of right and wrong that traditionally underpin criminology.

− Processes whereby discourses played out in society are not always described, but assumed.

− Self-surveillance has yet to be demonstrated as empirically grounded.

Synoptic links

To methodological issues

Zeitgeist The ideas of the time or the spirit of the age.

The lack of empirical grounding for much of the work of postmodernism is only partly due to its relatively recent development. The ideas that postmodernists present are difficult to put into practice in the real world. So, while they have a resonance with the *Zeitgeist* of the early twenty-first century, the evidence for their importance has yet to be confirmed. For example, postmodernists are hostile to most sociological research techniques, as they see them as sociologists' impositions on individuals and as incapable of identifying 'the truth' of a thing.

To other areas of the course

Issues of culture are important to postmodern sociologists and the notion of life styles has been used by them to categorise different segments of the population. This has a bearing on issues of crime and deviance, where the pursuit of a deviant or criminal lifestyle can be seen as a choice made by individuals in particular situations.

To theoretical issues

The challenge of postmodernism to traditional forms of sociology is one of the main theoretical debates going on in sociology, and crime and deviance form an important arena for debate. This is because the ideas associated with postmodernism have been explored in this area more than others, as the idea of a disciplinary society is so central to postmodernism's case. Issues of governance, including the control of crime, are a key component of postmodernism, which sees 'risk' as a main characteristic of the postmodern condition.

Examiner tip
Keep to the regular homework pattern established by your teachers, handing in work when it is due. Self-discipline helps you to prepare for the examination in good time.

Key concepts

discourse of progress, intensification of resentment, seduction, repression, surveillance, bio-power, disciplinary society

Key thinkers

Morrison, Denzin, Henry and Milovanovic, Bauman, Foucault

Summary

- There are many different approaches to the study of crime and deviance.
- Important aspects of that study include subcultures, social control, labelling and discourses.
- Realist approaches of the left and the right try to provide an account of crime that is as close to its actual manifestation as possible.
- More idealist approaches tend to see criminal activity in a more liberal light.
- Consensus theories emphasise the criminal's difference from the rest of society, while conflict theories tend to emphasise that crime occurs at all levels of society.
- Postmodern theories focus on the increasing surveillance that modern technologies and other developments have allowed to develop in society.

Explanations of the social distribution of crime and deviance and trends in crime

Definitions of crime and deviance and trends in crime

Key ideas

- The notion of deviance presupposes the existence of a 'normality' to which most people would subscribe and would recognise as such.
- Crime is sometimes defined as a sub-set of deviance, in that all criminal actions are seen as deviant, but not all deviant acts are illegal. However, even some crimes, such as smuggling a few cigarettes through customs, are largely accepted as not deviant.
- Even what is constituted as crime varies through time and space, with different societies having different notions of criminal actions and each society constantly changing its laws.
- Both crime and deviance are subject to social construction; that is, social processes that affect the inclusion or non-inclusion of actions as either deviant or criminal.
- Categories such as deviant are subject to discourses (ways of thinking and speaking about what it is possible to do and what it is not), such as scientific, moral and legal discourses. These change our conceptions of activities, depending on the **dominant discourse**.
- Definitions of crime have been extended to include the concept of the victim as an important player in the phenomenon of crime.
- Crime in Great Britain rose from the 1960s to a high in the early 1990s and has been declining since.
- Though showing some differences, crimes recorded by the police and crimes reported in the British Crime Survey show a broadly similar pattern over the last 50 years.
- Overall trends in crime may hide substantial shifts in specific crimes, such as crimes of violence.

Evaluation

+ There is a flexible approach to definitions that allows social change to be accounted for.

+ The categories of crime and deviance would be readily recognised by individuals, even if they could not agree on a definition.

Dominant discourse The way of thinking and speaking about what it is and is not possible to do in society that is supported by the state and by powerful groups in society.

Knowledge check 8

What other types of statistical source are often used by sociologists to describe patterns of crime in society?

+ We need to have definitions of crime in order to explore the causes of it and attempt to offer some solutions.

+ Crime statistics allow the sociologist to establish trends over time and patterns in the distribution of crime.

– It is argued that the category of deviance can have no meaning in a social world suffused with difference.

– The relativism of the category of crime in terms of time and space means that there can be little overall agreement on its causes.

– Some would argue that the above two points render the whole of the sociology of crime and deviance pointless.

– Much crime is invisible and unrecorded by the police, such as state crime.

Synoptic links

To methodological issues

When asking respondents about their attitudes towards crime and deviance, sociologists tend to assume that they all share a common understanding of what these are. However, it is not always the case that there are common definitions among respondents, and therefore they may be responding to questions, either in a questionnaire or an interview, with a different conception in mind.

To other areas of the course

The problems of defining crime and deviance are echoed in other areas of the course; for example when looking at the ways in which religion might be defined and the implications that different definitions have on the questions that sociologists ask about it.

To theoretical issues

The problem of relativism is a central one in sociological debates. The important aspect is whether or not the dependency of the definition of any concept on a particular time and place makes discussion of the phenomenon pointless.

Relativism This is in contrast to absolute truth and suggests that all knowledge is a product of its specific time or the specific groups or individuals who hold that knowledge to be true.

Key concepts

relativism, consensus, difference, social censure, normality, social construction, scientific discourse, crime explosion

Key thinkers

Durkheim, Sumner, Sykes, Hagan, Sparks

Official statistics

Key ideas

- Official statistics on crime are used extensively by sociologists as indicators of the amount and type of crime and the background of offenders, even though they cannot represent the 'real' rate of crime.
- Much crime is invisible, because crimes are under-reported for a number of reasons, including:
  - victims do not know a crime has been committed upon them
  - victims make the decision not to report a crime because of embarrassment or the trivial nature of the crime
  - decisions by the police to deal with crime unofficially rather than officially
  - the difficulty of detecting some crimes, especially financial frauds or deceptions
  - discretionary powers by the police and Crown Prosecution Service mean that many known crimes are not processed through the courts, but remain at the level of cautions or informal actions
- Official statistics on crime are therefore subject to processes of social construction in which social control agencies (mainly the police and the courts), victims, perpetrators and the public all have a role.
- Even where the statistics are accepted as robust, there are difficulties in interpreting them reliably.
- As laws change, public opinion about acceptable and unacceptable behaviour varies and there are fluctuations in the statistics that are the product of other social forces than just the rate of crime — for example, changes in policing practices.
- **Self-report surveys** and victim surveys suggest higher rates of crime than the official statistics, although these are also not without their problems.

Evaluation

+ The statistics provide a ready-made resource for sociologists interested in crime.

+ They show sufficient regularities and patterns across time to demonstrate something about the extent of reported crime.

+ They are used as guides for the formation of social policy in relation to crime by governments and social control agencies.

− The use of official statistics introduces systematic bias into the study of crime, stigmatising lower-class ethnic minority males in the inner city and ignoring huge amounts of white-collar and corporate crime.

− The social construction of such statistics means that they do not describe the real rate of crime and can lead to a fear of crime that is unrelated to an individual's actual risk of becoming a victim.

− Statistical correlations between crime and social factors can lead to simplistic explanations of the causes of crime and inappropriate measures to combat it.

Knowledge check 9

Identify one other formal social control agency.

Self-report surveys These result from when sociologists ask a sample to own up to crimes which they have committed whether they were caught or not.

Examiner tip
Watch television and films from a sociological point of view and try to apply appropriate concepts to the stories.

Synoptic links

To methodological issues

The use of official statistics to measure social phenomena is fraught with difficulty, and yet it is a most useful tool in describing and analysing large-scale trends and phenomena in society. However, there are limits to its usefulness. For example, when the 'counting rules' of the police change, there is discontinuity in comparing crimes across time.

To other areas of the course

The use of official statistics in many areas of sociology is a matter of controversy. Such statistics as birth and death rates are seen as 'hard' statistics — that is, robust and valid — while those to do with religious attendance are seen as 'soft'. Crime statistics, like the unemployment rate, are somewhere between these two.

To theoretical issues

Positivists are most likely to accept that the official statistics of crime represent a real social phenomenon worthy of sociological investigation, while interactionists would be more interested in the processes that lead to the social construction of the statistics and would reject the idea that they represented anything 'real'.

Counting rules The officially determined guidelines for what should and should not be included when reporting the numbers of detected crimes to the government.

Key concepts

patterned regularities, bias, social construction, under-reporting, invisibility, selective law enforcement, self-report studies

Key thinkers

Mirrlees-Black, British Crime Survey, Box, Morrison, Croall

Social class

Key ideas

- The official statistics on crime represent a real concentration of criminal activity in the working class and a relative absence of criminal behaviour among the middle and upper classes.
- Explanations for this distribution include:
  - the material and social conditions of the working class, including levels of employment, material deprivation and marginalisation from mainstream society
  - a focus on the characteristics of the working class itself, including such factors as the norms and values it holds, which include hedonism and a search for excitement and machismo

Knowledge check 10

What is meant by 'machismo'?

- a subculture of risk taking and positive attitudes towards breaking the law, and poor socialisation into moral constraints against law breaking
- weak levels of control, both in terms of individual self-control among working-class criminals and of social control, in terms of the penalties used to punish wrong doing
- the demise of working-class communities with strong communal links that acted to deter potential law-breakers. Capitalism generates economic outcasts (often unemployed), who have to turn to crime to survive in a hostile world
- the activities of the social control agencies stigmatise the working class and produce statistics that bear little relation to the real distribution of crime

- Increasingly, crime is concentrated in an 'underclass' of the 'undeserving poor', characterised by lone-parent families, poor socialisation and the collapse of traditional moral values.
- The levels of violence and other deviant/criminal activity, such as drug taking, are significantly higher among the lower classes.

Stigmatise To label individuals or groups with marginalising or excluding characteristics.

Evaluation

+ Official statistics consistently demonstrate that most crime is carried out by lower-class individuals on other lower-class individuals.

+ Allows a concentration of resources on those areas most subject to criminal and deviant activity.

+ A combination of factors could explain this concentration and help develop social policies to deal with the problem.

− The emphasis on the working class allows society to turn a blind eye to criminal activity in other social classes.

− Several of the explanations come close to 'victim blaming' and stigmatising large sections of the working class, when the majority is law abiding.

− The distribution of deviant activity, such as drug taking, is not class-concentrated but is ubiquitous. However, the target for policing these issues is the working class.

Examiner tip
As you go through your other topics on the course, note in the margins any connections that might be made to the issue of crime and deviance. For example, if you are studying power and politics, you might note that crime is an issue of some importance in political debates between the parties.

Synoptic links

To methodological issues

Studies that rely on official statistics for their examination of the **class distribution** of crime and deviance have to contend with the fact that they are socially constructed, and also that they consistently show that crime is concentrated in a certain class, both as perpetrators and as victims. Official statistics do not get behind the real meaning of crime for both offenders and victims.

Class distribution The patterns of occurrence and non-occurrence of phenomena between the working class, middle class and upper class.

To other areas of the course

There are clear links between stratification theories and the focus of research in crime and deviance on the working class. It is the subordinate position of the working class in both material and ideological terms that partly accounts for the way in which it is targeted by sociologists.

To theoretical issues

Different explanations are drawn from different traditions within sociology, so that interactionists do not see the 'crime and class' problem in the same way that Marxists do. The influence of the domain assumptions of these approaches needs to be explored when studying crime and deviance.

Key concepts

culture, subculture, material conditions, marginalisation, control, labelling, policing policies, capitalism as crimogenic

Key thinkers

Braithwaite, Shaw and McKay, Miller, Wolfgang and Ferracuti, Taylor, Morrison

Crimes of the powerful

Key ideas

- Crime and deviance are spread fairly evenly throughout the class structure — it is just that lower class offenders tend to be caught and processed as criminals more often than middle-class offenders.
- White-collar crime (committed by middle-class workers) merges into corporate crime.
- Occupational crime is that committed by white-collar workers for personal gain, corporate crime is illegal activity commissioned or sanctioned by individuals for corporate gain.
- White-collar crime causes large financial losses to organisations, but is relatively under-investigated by the social control agencies.
- Much corporate crime is extremely harmful to individuals and communities and is committed because of pressure on executives to cut costs, and therefore corners, in order to maximise profits.
- The boundaries between organised crime and respectable large corporations are becoming increasingly blurred.

Knowledge check 11

What is the difference between corporate crime and white-collar crime?

Corporate crime Illegal activity carried out by employees of organisations, usually in pursuit of profit.

Examiner tip
Do any reading that your teacher asks you to do and try to do some of your own, focusing on what particularly interests you about a topic.

Evaluation

+ Redresses the balance by drawing attention to criminal activity other than that of the working class.

+ Offers a fuller account of the distribution of criminal activity in society.

+ Promotes the investigation of events that may have powerful negative effects on individuals and communities.

– There is a tendency to exaggerate the extent and the effects of corporate crime.

– It is argued that there are strong social and legal pressures on business executives not to commit crimes.

– Corporate crimes in particular are hard to explore with any degree of direct evidence, due to the secretive nature of most corporations.

Synoptic links

To methodological issues

There are immense difficulties in penetrating the activities of corporations, even when investigating legal activities. For a consideration of their illegal activities, sociologists have to rely mainly on **secondary data**, such as media stories and government reports. For primary data they may rely on 'whistle-blowers', who have their own methodological difficulties. Those who report the illegal activities of others may have their own motivations for doing so, other than a desire to see the law upheld. For example, they may be jealous, vengeful, ambitious or driven by ideology. It would be difficult to investigate the crimes of the powerful by interview or questionnaire if they were resistant to investigation. Only some form of covert method might work in such circumstances.

Secondary data Information that has not been collected by sociologists but by other individuals and organisations for non-sociological purposes.

To other areas of the course

The illegal activities of corporate bodies can be linked to the study of work and leisure. Most studies in the sociology of work tend to focus on the routine activities of organisations, and the theorists of corporate crime are suggesting that many executives routinely commit criminal acts in the pursuit of profit.

To theoretical issues

While many of the sociologists investigating white-collar crime are drawn from the functionalist tradition of sociology, those interested in corporate crime are usually associated with conflict and Marxist approaches. There are consequently dangers of bias in these approaches.

Key concepts

white-collar crime, corporate crime, occupational crime, state criminality, amoral calculators

Key thinkers

Sutherland, Coleman, Buss, Chambliss, Kramer, Pearce and Tombs

Age

Key ideas

- Crime and deviant activities are mainly carried out by the young, especially those between the ages of 14 and 24, and the majority of victims are also in the same age bracket.
- The main interest of young people is self-gratification, which can lead to feelings of indifference to others, even those who are the potential victims of their actions.
- Not all young people are deviant or criminal, and much depends on the strength of their personal networks that connect them to mainstream society, such as family, peers, school and community. The stronger the bonds, the less likely it is that the young will be involved in criminal actions.
- Those that do commit crime or deviant acts employ 'techniques of neutralisation' that allow them to suspend their normal commitment to obeying the law, through 'explaining away' their actions.
- Being involved in criminal or deviant activity requires a calculation by the young that the material gain, or excitement of the feeling of being in control, outweighs the potential of discovery and capture by the agents of social control.
- While most young criminals 'grow out' of their illegal activities as they settle down to family responsibilities, they continue to demonstrate a lack of self-control in their lives — for example, through heavy drinking.
- Young 'rebels' against the system form deviant subcultures that express their opposition to mainstream society through particular styles, often designed to shock or express difference.
- The lifestyles of the young are more likely to expose them to greater risk of victimisation, or greater opportunity to engage in deviant or criminal behaviour.

Evaluation

+ The focus on the young reflects the statistical and common sense views of where crime and deviance is concentrated.

+ Explanations seek to establish both the opportunities for young people to engage in illegal activity and their motivations for doing so, in the context of the social situation in which they find themselves.

Knowledge check 12

Suggest one technique of neutralisation.

Agents of social control Institutions that seek to establish social order, formally as in the case of the police, or less formally, as with the family.

Examiner tip

Use the internet as often as you can. There are some excellent sites dedicated to A-level sociology and more general sociological sites that will stretch your sociological imagination.

+ Changes over time are included, as theorists seek to explain the transition of the young from being at the margins of society to adopting mainstream lifestyles.

– The focus on the young leads to a neglect of the criminality of other age groups.

– Much illegal activity of the young is transitory, opportunistic and mundane.

– 'Rebellion' is a 'natural', not deviant, condition for young people as they seek to establish their own identities.

Synoptic links

To methodological issues

For sociologists, who tend to be slightly older than the young people they are investigating, gaining entry to their social worlds can be problematic. Nevertheless, several sociologists have secured membership of young people's gangs, but the validity and reliability of the data they have collected are open to debate.

To other areas of the course

Young people, in various guises or subcultural styles, often form a 'folk devil' for older people. Their stigmatisation is based on nostalgia for a 'lost world' of order and conformity, which has never actually existed. This yearning for a stable past is reinforced through media representations.

To theoretical issues

While most perspectives offer different views on the causes and consequences of young people's engagement in criminal activity, they seem at first sight to be united in assuming that there is a concentration of criminality in the young. The importance of this (whether it is transitory or deep-seated, mundane or serious) is what separates these perspectives.

Key concepts

moral symmetry, network analysis, techniques of neutralisation, deviant subculture, style

Key thinkers

Hough and Mayhew, Schwendinger and Schwendinger, Bartol and Bartol, Box, Matza, Gottfredson and Hirschi, CCCS

Social world In contrast to the natural world, this is the environment that is built up by the actions and interactions of individuals and groups, creating a distinctly constructed world.

Locality

Key ideas

- Cities are the main locality for the commissioning of crime, while rural areas remain relatively crime-free.
- Certain areas of cities exhibit social characteristics associated with high levels of crime and deviance, such as high levels of geographical mobility, family instability, unemployment and poor living accommodation.
- In urban areas with existing adult criminal enterprises, young people are more likely to engage in crime themselves. In areas without such illegitimate opportunities, young people drift into gang activity or retreatist subcultures based around drugs.
- Cities generate an underclass that has rejected the discourse of progress and that therefore poses a major threat to social order in the city, either through its criminal activity or by its propensity to engage in social disorder.
- Urban crime increases as globalisation dissolves the city's manufacturing base, which constitutes the basis for community life in inner city areas.
- Poor urban communities lose their sense of space and identity traditionally associated with the inner city as warehouses and industrial land are given over to expensive flats and gentrification.
- Deindustrialisation of the city creates a group of long-term isolated males, who turn to burglary and violence to replace the welfare benefits that have been squeezed by successive governments.

Evaluation

+ There are clear correlations between certain urban areas and levels of crime.

+ Addresses the concentration of poor conditions in certain areas of cities as a cause of crime.

+ Looks at global developments and their effect on urban localities.

− Based on a dichotomy between urban and rural areas that is too rigid.

− Not all areas with high levels of social disorganisation exhibit high crime rates.

− Pattern of crime in urban areas is related as much to the pattern of policing as to a greater propensity to commit crime — i.e. individuals in the inner city are more likely to get caught.

Synoptic links

To methodological issues

The relationship of global processes to local developments is one that involves a high level of sociological imagination in making the connections between the two levels, as well as a detailed analysis of developments in the world economy and events in small localities. Because of the subject matter in this area, traditional research instruments are difficult to employ.

Geographical mobility The movement of individuals and groups between places, such as the shift from rural to urban living or the drift of population to the southern parts of Great Britain.

Knowledge check 13

What do you understand by deindustrialisation?

Examiner tip

When making crime and deviance notes, take care to record where your teacher draws attention to any synoptic links.

Community A type of social organisation in which members strongly identify with one another and exhibit feelings of solidarity with each other.

To other areas of the course

There is an important connection to be made between studies of crime and deviance in urban areas and the study of community values and practices. The absence of a sense of community in urban areas is often seen as one of the causes of criminal activity.

To theoretical issues

The increased fracturing of cities has been one of the main interests of postmodern sociologists, who are attracted to the idea of a dissolving, uncertain, diverse environment, such as the city, as a metaphor for postmodern living.

Key concepts

social disorganisation, illegitimate opportunity structures, retreatism, globalisation, deindustrialisation

Key thinkers

Park, Burgess, Shaw and McKay, Cloward and Ohlin, Morrison, Petras and Davenport

Gender

Key ideas

- The apparently lower incidence of crime among women cannot be explained solely in terms of biological differences between men and women.
- Explanations of this phenomenon have included:
  - girls are socialised differently from boys to accept a more passive, less risk-taking public persona
  - women do not have the same freedoms in society as men and therefore have fewer opportunities to commit crime
  - the social penalties for deviant behaviour by women (such as getting pregnant while young) are greater than for men
  - women have a greater awareness of the risk of arrest and therefore calculate avoidance strategies
- Crime among women is claimed to be rising for the following reasons:
  - changes in the social roles of women have led to an equality of opportunity to commit crime
  - feminism has transformed the way that women see themselves and their needs, so that they are more inclined to seek gratification of material wants through illegal activity

Avoidance strategies Patterns of behaviour which seek to minimise the risk to an individual or group, for example, not going out in the dark.

Knowledge check 14

Name one other crime that women are more likely to be involved in.

- the marginal position of women in the economic market place makes them more predisposed to economic crimes, particularly ethnic minority women
- The search for equivalence has led to a focus on crimes of violence perpetrated by the 'mean girl'.
- Women are more likely to be the victims of crime than perpetrators and are particularly vulnerable to sexual and domestic violence.
- Women commit different types of crime from men, being more likely to shoplift, for example.
- Some argue that it is not that women are less criminally inclined but it is the way that statistics are compiled and the way that the police and courts deal with women offenders that leads to a greater invisibility of female crime.
- A focus on masculinity suggests that images of what it means to be male are under pressure as the traditional bread-winning role of the man is reduced, leading to a crisis in masculinity that manifests itself in greater violence.

Examiner tip

Before you start your revision, make sure that you are aware of what the specification requires for the examination.

Evaluation

+ Reduces the invisibility of women on the sociological agenda.

+ Recognises the importance of female experiences both as criminals and as victims.

+ Locates explanations in the social and ideological relationships in society.

− If there is going to be a full understanding of the issues, it is important to remember that explanations of gender and crime have to be tied in with factors such as social class and ethnicity.

− Tends to treat the female experience as an undifferentiated whole, rather than seeing different groups of women as having different experiences of crime and deviance.

− Work on masculinity is undeveloped.

Synoptic links

To methodological issues

The idea of the invisibility of women from sociological discourse has been paralleled by female absence from empirical studies. It has only relatively recently been the case that feminists have begun to define what a feminist methodology would look like and how it would be employed to explore the female experience of crime. Traditional research instruments, such as the questionnaire or interview, can be affected by the gender of the researcher.

To other areas of the course

Clearly, this focus on women, men, crime and deviance has a part to play in looking at gender differences in society, particularly in terms of the theme of stratification and differentiation.

Invisibility The tendency for groups or individuals to be absent from the sociological gaze, usually because of a marginalised position or because other groups or individuals are conceptualised as more important.

To theoretical issues

Feminism as a perspective is one of the most important approaches to the study of female crime and deviance and you should be aware of the different strands within it, and how each strand has approached the issues.

Key concepts

patriarchy, sex roles, public/private spheres, malestream sociology, hegemony, hegemonic masculinities, search for equivalence, 'mean girls'

Key thinkers

Sutherland, Leonard, Steffensmeier and Allen, Heidensohn, Messerschmidt, Chesney-Lynd

Ethnicity

Key ideas

- The relationship between crime rates and ethnicity is extremely complex, due to factors such as the difficulties of identifying ethnic origin and the cultural and social differences between ethnic groups.
- Ethnic minority males are over-represented in the crime statistics, compared to their proportion in the population, and this has been explained by a number of factors:
  - one view suggests that there is a greater disposition towards crime among ethnic minorities for varied reasons
  - others argue that the activities of the police target ethnic minorities more, leading to greater arrest rates among these groups
  - a third view suggests that racist stereotypes in 'cop culture' have the effect of over-representing ethnic minorities in arrest figures
- Explanations for 'black criminality' include:
  - the greater economic deprivation of minority ethnic communities leads to frustration, greater levels of violence and crime
  - the social isolation by residential segregation of some ethnic communities from mainstream society leads to the development of a subculture that is more disposed to crime
  - the lack of community networks as a result of immigration leads to unsupervised minority ethnic youth activity, which can lean towards the deviant and criminal
- Public, police and judicial bias against ethnic minorities ensures that there are hostile encounters with those ethnic minorities caught in criminal justice processes, so outcomes are more likely to result in blacks being labelled as criminals.

Over-representation
The incidence of phenomena in a group is greater than what is expected given the proportion of the group in the general population.

Knowledge check 15

What is meant by social capital?

- Ethnic minorities comprise a large proportion of the underclass, with a concentration effect, so that the social control of the urban environment where they live is seen as necessary for public order.
- The lack of social capital in the form of strong community links can undermine communal censure of drug taking, with the result that there are high levels of use among some ethnic minorities.
- Ethnic minorities are also more likely to be the victims of crime disproportionate to their numbers, and this is particularly so for ethnic minority women.

Evaluation

+ The focus on ethnicity allows a consideration of the differential experience of ethnic groups in society.

+ Recognition that there is a complex relationship between the statistics of 'black crime' and reality on the streets.

+ It identifies drugs and violence as problems for ethnic communities themselves.

− There is a danger that ethnic minorities may be seen as 'naturally' disposed towards crime.

− Research in this area may reinforce the more negative stereotypes that the ethnic minorities and the police may have of each other.

− It is difficult to isolate the effects of the various factors that interplay in the study of ethnicity and crime and deviance.

Examiner tip
Be active in your revision strategies — don't just sit and read your notes. Try to do exercises and activities that test your AO2 skills.

Synoptic links

To methodological issues

The lumping together of different social groups into a single category ('black' or 'ethnic minority') results in a distortion of the social reality of the various components. This methodological issue has implications for social policy and the way that ethnic minorities are seen by agents of social control.

To other areas of the course

Ethnicity, along with class and gender, forms the backbone of the theme of stratification and differentiation, which runs throughout the specification. In addition, the issues of culture and identity (the second theme) are also important in seeking to explain the statistics of crime and deviance.

To theoretical issues

The study of ethnicity is closely connected to differing perspectives, ranging from the assimilationist views current in the 1960s, through multicultural perspectives of the 1970s, the anti-racist views of the 1980s and ideas about new racism in the 1990s.

Assimilation The process whereby migrant communities change to become as much like the host community as possible.

Key concepts

hard policing, racism, 'cop culture', marginalisation, other, new racism

Key thinkers

Taylor, Lea and Young, Gilroy, Wilson, Sampson and Laub, Arrigo

Summary

So far this topic has looked at definitions and frequency of crime and explanations of the social distribution of crime. The key points you need to know include:

- The definition and frequency of criminal activity are not easy to establish, as definitions change according to time and culture and official statistics do not capture the totality of crime.
- Much criminology has examined the apparent concentration of crime in the lower classes, including an underclass and neglected its occurrence among the upper and middle classes.
- Young people are disproportionately represented in the criminal statistics and sociologists have tended to see crime as a youthful phenomenon.
- In urban areas, crime appears to be more frequent and violent than in rural areas.
- Explanations of ethnic minority criminal activity have tended to focus on their social location in areas of deprivation.
- Lower, but rising levels of crime among women have renewed sociological interest in the female criminal.

Contemporary issues in the sociology of crime

Globalisation and crime

Key ideas

- Corporate crime is increasingly taking on a global dimension as organisations gain the ability to move large amounts of money, staff and expertise swiftly around the world.
- Organised criminal activity has expanded into 'global trades', based on drug trafficking, the sex trade, people trafficking and money laundering.
- Costs of global crime are unknown but estimated to be enormous.
- The internet has allowed the development of new forms of global crime — called cybercrime — including hacking, scams and frauds.
- The internet allows 'old' crimes, such as fraud, to take place on a broader basis, as well as new forms of crime.
- Virtual reality allows identity to be hidden.

Cybercrime Any illegal activity that utilises computers and the internet as the locus of the activity.

- International terrorist groups not only commit global crimes themselves, but also cooperate globally with organised crime to raise funds for terrorist activities.
- The crime–terror continuum can take several forms and it is often difficult to disentangle the terrorist from the purely money-motivated crime.
- Global crime is difficult to police because the law lags behind new offences. It is not always clear where the crime was committed and so who is responsible for detection.
- The emergence of global crime has driven the forces of law and order to cooperate internationally and employ increasingly sophisticated computer programs to combat it.

Evaluation

+ It shifts the focus to an increasingly important aspect of criminal activity.

+ It touches upon contemporary concerns about terror and the misuse of the internet.

+ Sociologists can develop new tools and analyses in exploring these global phenomena.

– By their nature, these forms of crime are difficult to research in a scientific way.

– The focus on the global can obscure what concerns most people about crime in their daily lives — that is, low-intensity incivilities.

– Important aspects of global crime may be ignored or sidelined through a concentration on cybercrime and terrorism.

Synoptic links

To methodological issues

The secretive nature of global criminal and/or terrorist groups makes them impermeable to traditional methods of research. Much of the information that can be gleaned about such activities is secondary in nature.

To other areas of the course

The clearest link is to the sociology of politics, where the activities of terrorist groups in pursuit of political ends is a key element of a contemporary sociology of pressure groups. The blurring of the boundaries between terrorism and criminal gangs makes this a fruitful area of investigation in both topics

To theoretical issues

The most likely approach to be adopted towards these issues is some form of conflict theory. Through the issues of risk and uncertainty, there are also connections to be made between postmodern theory and the nature of global terrorism.

Knowledge check 16

What is meant by a continuum in sociology?

Examiner tip

Always carry out the **MOT test** to establish synoptic links at every opportunity. That is, you need to make connections to the:

- **M**ethods that sociologists use (this is central to your ability to answer question 03)
- **O**ther areas of the course
- **T**heories that sociologists employ

Pressure groups These act collectively to promote a particular cause or idea or to defend the interests of their members.

Key concepts

transnational organised crime (TOC), cybercrime, terror–crime continuum, borderless world, black-hole syndrome

Key thinkers

Held, Gross, Capeller, Grabosky, Holmes, Makerenko

The mass media and crime: deviancy amplification

Key ideas

- Most people's perceptions of crime are obtained from media reports.
- There is a tendency for the media to sensationalise events and unusual social groups, so that these come to be seen by the public as 'folk devils' — a phenomenon about which 'something must be done'.
- The reactions of the social control agencies to this moral panic lead to over-policing, with the effect that more criminal activity by the social group is detected.
- Those labelled as folk devils often play up to their image in the media, thus creating a self-fulfilling prophecy of a dangerous deviant group.
- The spiral of events, exaggeration and reaction continues until the media lose interest in the group or the focus shifts to other sensational events.
- Moral panics may be 'manufactured' by special interests to further their own agenda.
- Governments may use moral panics about terrorism to promote laws that curtail freedoms.
- The more complex structure of the media (with the growth of the internet) makes the establishment of folk devils more problematic because of the variety of sources of information.
- Social reality for the majority is composed of the way that the media mediate information about the wider social world.

Evaluation

+ It is a useful model for exploring the issues of 'crime waves' and the 'fear of crime'.

+ It establishes the centrality of the media as a source of information and imagery about events and people beyond the individual's immediate experience.

+ It links the forces of social control with both the public and members of the deviant subcultures.

Folk devils Stereotyped groups in society who are stigmatised as having some anti-social dimension to them and become a 'cause for concern'.

Knowledge check 17

Suggest one group that has been labelled as a folk devil.

Examiner tip

Organise your revision by establishing a timetable for the 2 months before the examination.

– Those who seek to influence the course of public debate about a social group or social issue are much more diverse than just the media, though most will engage with the media as they seek to persuade the public of the rightness of their views.

– Members of deviant subcultures have a more complex relationship with the media, often using it to spread knowledge about their lifestyle choices.

– Unless there is real concern in the general public about an issue, then scapegoating is difficult to accomplish.

Synoptic links

To methodological issues

One of the main methodological techniques used by sociologists of deviancy amplification is content analysis of media reports. They chart the rise and portrayal of folk devils in the media, and compare them to the public response to the representations depicted. It is the nature of the subject matter that makes this technique so appropriate.

To other areas of the course

The obvious link in this section is to the mass media, which operates as the main vehicle for deviancy amplification.

To theoretical issues

The notion of deviancy amplification emerges firmly from the interactionist school of sociology and particularly from work on labelling. Realist critics of this approach suggest that it implies that the actions of the folk devils are in some sense harmless or trivial, even when they include violence.

Labelling Agents of social control attach stereotypes to social groups or individuals that have (usually negative) consequences for those so labelled.

Key concepts

folk devils, moral panics, stereotyping, stigmatisation, media representation, manufacture of moral panics

Key thinkers

Cohen, McRobbie and Thornton, Taylor, Haltom and McCann

Green crime

Key ideas

- The focus on the environment emerges from a wider definition of crime and deviance that includes 'social harm', rather than just law breaking or going against social norms.
- In its broadest sense, this includes not just harm committed against the environment, but also harm against all living things.
- Encompasses the activities of powerful institutions such as transnational corporations and the cumulative activities of millions of individuals, whose way of life impacts upon the environment.
- Green criminology has a wide remit and can include a large number of legal and illegal actions.
- Interests range from food crimes (adulteration), animal rights (vivisection), waste disposal (legal and illegal dumping) to EU fishing policies.
- There is a major division between those sociologists who focus on environmental hazards to classes of the population and those who concentrate on the effects of humanity on the biosphere.
- Because of the nature of the interest, green sociologists tend to take a more global view of issues affecting the environment.

Evaluation

+ Focuses on conditions that affect everyone in the world and that could have larger-scale consequences arising from inaction.

+ By using the idea of 'social harm', it extends the interests of sociologists into areas previously ignored.

+ In looking at the international actions of powerful institutions, it acts as a brake on their illegal activity and questions many of their legal activities through lobbying for changes in international laws.

− The remit of environmental criminology is so wide that it can hardly be said to be an area of criminology at all, but of environmental politics.

− The work of the green criminologists has had little impact on the practices of the powerful institutions that they challenge.

− The whole area is controversial, with limited consensus as to what constitutes good practice even over seemingly straightforward issues such as the vivisection of animals.

Synoptic links

To methodological issues

The main issue to consider here is the nature of the subject matter itself. Not only is much of the work of green sociology imbued with moral considerations (and

---

Transnational corporations
Businesses that operate in many areas of the world and whose activities are not restricted to a particular nation-state, though their headquarters are. Also known as multinationals.

Knowledge check 18
Give an example of the effect of humanity on the biosphere.

Examiner tip
Review your notes at regular intervals.

Moral considerations
Ethical issues raised by whatever is under consideration.

---

therefore difficult for any research technique to be employed in an unbiased way), but also many methods would not access the areas where real power over these issues lies.

To other areas of the course

As a relatively 'new' area of sociological concern, the links to other areas of the course are limited. However, green sociologists do draw on many concepts associated with stratification and differentiation when considering the environmental hazards facing different groups in the world. With its global interest, there are also connections to be made to global development.

To theoretical issues

Green sociologists are drawn from a wide range of perspectives, but they tend to take a critical stance towards current practices and social actions.

Key concepts

eco-crime, food crimes, anthropocentric, environmental justice, ecological justice

Key thinkers

Lynch and Stretesky, Situ and Evans, Munroe

Human rights and state crimes

Key ideas

- Governments also commit crimes, and increasingly so in a world in which human rights legislation has gained legitimacy in many countries.
- Human rights legislation forms the basis of many states' activities in a global context and, in transgressing the rights of their own citizens or those of other nations, states can be guilty of criminal behaviour.
- State crimes are, therefore, any crimes committed by governments or their agents either directly, complicitly or through inaction.
- State crimes can take many forms of social harm, from corruption, to state terrorism, through to war crimes and genocide.
- Terrorism after the Second World War was often state sponsored, as in the anti-colonial struggles in the under-developed world, and can still be so in 'failed states'.
- It is often difficult to establish whether a state has actually committed crimes as there are disagreements over the legal status of specific actions, such as the invasion of Iraq to topple Saddam Hussein.
- Arguments about state crime are inevitably bound up with political issues and positions that individuals take for or against particular actions.

Human rights A concept that was developed to suggest that everyone, as a result of their common humanity, is entitled to the same fair and just treatment wherever they might be located in the world.

Knowledge check 19

Which organisation has responsibility for establishing the legality of actions by states to interfere in the affairs of other states?

- It is particularly difficult to show that inaction by a state has resulted in criminal social harm.
- Where states are accused of committing crime, they use their powerful resources to promote different 'strategies of denial'.
- States may also use terrorist activity as a device to raise levels of fear in populations, so that dilutions in human rights can take place legally.

Evaluation

+ There is a welcome shift away from petty criminality to the much more potentially harmful activities of states.

+ The area addresses one of the biggest issues that face the contemporary world — international terrorism and the response of states to it within a human rights framework.

+ Work in this area illuminates the more secretive areas of social life at opposite ends of the scale — government and anti-governmental terrorist groups.

- It is impossible to agree on what actually constitutes a state crime, even when there are human rights breaches, as the national interest can always be brought into play.

- The area of study is often ethnocentric, assuming that it is states in the under-developed world that are more likely to be corrupt or use state terror tactics on resisting citizens.

- Human rights laws are themselves controversial, as they include provisions that some do not perceive as 'natural' human rights.

> **Examiner tip**
> Subscribe to *Sociology Review* and access back copies held by your school or college library. It is one of the best sources of contemporary sociological work in the areas you will be examined on.

> **Freedom of information** The idea that, as taxpayers pay for the actions of governments and their agents, then information about what governments do should be available to those taxpayers.

> **Synoptic links**

To methodological issues

By their nature, these issues are difficult to investigate and there is a reliance on secondary material to explore the global activities of states. While many state papers are open to **freedom of information** action, many are kept secret in the 'national interest'.

To other areas of the course

The clear link here is to global development — the role of states in promoting or undermining development is a central one.

To theoretical issues

The idea of 'state crime' raises many definitional problems and some would argue that there is no such thing, even under international law, as the state is an entity and not an individual.

Key concepts

state crimes, war crimes, genocide, strategies of denial, war on terror, privatisation of terror

Key thinkers

Green and Ward, Cohen, Hajjar, Hamm, Welch

This topic has now looked at globalisation and crime, the mass media and crime, green crime and human rights and states crimes. The key points you need to know include:

- The development of a global economy has led to an increasing sociological interest in the emergence of global crime, either through the activities of transnational corporations or through organised crime's involvement in drugs and people smuggling.

- There has also been an increase in sociological interest in crimes against the environment and the biosphere, using the idea of 'social harm'.
- The acceptance of state crimes in an era of human rights legislation has widened the scope of criminology's interests.
- The activities of the mass media are an important factor in the representation of crime and criminals in people's minds and can have social control effects.

Summary

The criminal justice system

Police, crime and deviance

Key ideas

- The police have enormous power in society but the norms of policing lead to under-enforcement, as officers use their powers of discretion to keep the peace rather than just enforce the law.
- 'Cop culture' shapes the ways in which the police deal with different segments of the public and the police are sometimes accused of being sexist, racist and homophobic.
- The policing policy adopted (community policing, rapid response, paramilitary policing, zero tolerance) is important in defining who gets targeted and how suspects are treated, once apprehended.
- Policing tends to be concentrated on members of the underclass and the places where they live because 'cop culture' identifies the poor as the most law-breaking section of the community.
- Policing activities are not always cost-effective in the fight against crime, as there is a symbiotic relationship between police and crime.

Knowledge check 20

What do you understand by zero tolerance policing?

Symbolic power The idea that something has a strong hold over the beliefs and activities of individuals in society, in contrast to force or coercion.

- A major role of the police continues to be the maintenance of social order, rather than just catching criminals.
- The privatisation of security is a feature of postmodern societies as private firms become involved in activities traditionally carried out by the state.
- This has coincided with the emergence of a culture of control, of which 'the public must be protected' is a basic principle.
- Police retain considerable symbolic power in society, often being seen as a bulwark against disorder and anarchy.

Evaluation

+ The police retain the affection of the public in the fight against crime.

+ The police do respond to the mood of the public for different forms of policing.

+ The everyday activities of the police are multi-faceted and varied.

− Differential policing of communities leads to feelings of oppression among the most policed.

− 'Cop culture' discourages the participation of women, ethnic minorities and gays in the policing of society.

− Privatised security firms are not subject to the same controls as the police.

Examiner tip
Produce reduced versions of your notes that will help you to revise later on.

Synoptic links

To methodological issues

The investigation of the police's activities is affected by many ethical considerations. While there are many television programmes devoted to fictional and real policing, sociologists find that it is hard to carry out observation of real police activity because of the involvement of the criminal and victim.

To other areas of the course

Occupational culture All the common actions, beliefs and values of those who carry out the same line of work.

Policing is an occupation like any other and the notion of an occupational culture, drawn from the sociology of work, is important in explaining how the police go about their work.

To theoretical issues

The investigation of policing has been carried out by many different types of sociologist who focus on different aspects, depending on their theoretical point of view. So, functionalists are interested in the value consensus of the police as they go about their work, while conflict theorists are more focused on police relationships in subordinating communities.

Key concepts

'cop culture', zero tolerance, community policing, privatisation of policing, police voice, culture of control

Key thinkers

Banton, Chambliss, Skogan, Morgan, Reiner, Wilson and Kelling, Gardner

Law, crime and deviance

Key ideas

- Law is seen by conflict theorists as a key way in which powerful groups in society seek to maintain their hold over less powerful groups.
- Marxists argue that the law is directly a tool of the ruling class, used to criminalise those sections of society that might challenge its control and to legitimise its own actions in the pursuit of profit.
- Law for the functionalists represents the accumulated wisdom of a society, which is passed on from generation to generation.
- Postmodernists argue that the law is always a transient set of rules, which is distributed throughout the whole of social life and not just contained in the legal system.
- The law is only one part of a surveillance society.
- The notion of the law can also act as an ideology, used to justify the actions of governments and their agents in defence of it.
- The New Right sees the law as the central means of controlling the activities of a criminal underclass.

Evaluation

+ Sociologists link the law to other social and economic systems, rather than treating it as a separate entity.

+ The role of the law in maintaining social order and accomplishing social control is established.

+ Postmodernists show that the law is only one of a large number of ways in which power can be expressed in postmodern societies.

- Marxists offer a 'conspiracy theory' of the law, indicating that it serves mainly the interests of the ruling class.

- Functionalists assume that the law represents wisdom rather than being the outcome of struggle between different interests in society.

- The law is not only ideological but also represents a material practice in society associated with ideas such as justice and fairness.

> **Knowledge check 21**
> What is the Marxist term for the ruling class?

> **Surveillance society**
> A situation in which the activities of individuals are subject to the mundane, everyday exercise of power, so that individuals act as if they are being watched all the time.

> **Examiner tip**
> Review your notes and note in the margin where other synoptic links might be. Use a different colour for links to other parts of the course: to sociological methods and to sociological theories.

Synoptic links

To methodological issues

The law is represented as an abstract body of knowledge and is therefore largely open to investigation only through secondary materials.

To other areas of the course

The law frames much of social life — for example, religions are regulated through the law, establishing the Church of England as the church of the British state. It also establishes the limits of acceptable religious practice for all religions and sects; for example, through its defence of monogamy.

To theoretical issues

The divisions between different perspectives on the role of the law stand as an exemplar of the disputes that characterise sociological approaches. Each sociological perspective has its unique view of the nature and function of the law.

Monogamy The legally established practice whereby one woman and one man only are allowed to be married at any particular time.

Key concepts

ideological construction, law and order ideology, law as a weapon, justice

Key thinkers

Turk, Scraton, Cavadino and Dignan, Moore

Prevention, punishment and the criminal justice system

Key ideas

Knowledge check 22

What does CCTV stand for?

- Target-hardening initiatives (CCTV, security doors in blocks of flats etc.) reduce opportunities for criminals to commit crimes but may displace such activities into softer target areas.
- The courts and prison service are responsive to changes in public attitudes towards crime and criminals, but also retain a distinctive view of the nature of justice and punishment.
- The criminal justice system is increasingly influenced by the concept of 'risk' in determining its policies towards convicted criminals.
- As the state seeks to control society in an increasingly fractured and disordered world, criminal justice agencies in a postmodern society classify populations, rather than individuals, as highly likely to commit crime.

- Marxists see the prison system as a source of cheap labour and as a reserve army, with correspondence between the organisation of factories and the organisation of prisons.
- Foucauldian approaches see new initiatives in punishment policies (towards less imprisonment and more community sentencing) as more subtle ways of establishing control over dissident populations.
- Half-way punishments, such as community sentences, have the effect of widening the net for those caught up in the criminal justice system as they constitute a cheaper way of punishing offenders than a prison sentence.
- The respect agenda and strategies such as the use of ASBOs are early intervention strategies to try and deal with incivilities in communities.
- There is a new punitiveness in public attitudes towards punishment as a result of media highlighting of 'crime waves' and an increased fear of crime.
- Incapacitation theory argues that putting people in prison is not a deterrent, but it prevents them from offending while they are inside, and this is sufficient justification for incarceration.
- Governments may use 'fear of crime' as a technology of governance to persuade the public that ever harsher punishments are needed.

Reserve army A Marxist term that suggests that certain sectors of the population are recruited in and out of work as suits capitalist activity and function to keep wages low and workers disciplined.

Evaluation

+ Focus on criminal justice system is relatively new and fills a gap in our understanding of crime and deviance.

+ Encompasses a number of central issues in contemporary society such as justice and punishment.

+ Linked to practical ideas for improving the efficiency of the criminal justice system and combating crime.

− Tends to assert the importance of the idea of risk rather than showing it to be important.

− Policies concerning prison that are put forward can have real and detrimental effects without necessarily being shown to reduce crime.

Issues of cost effectiveness are often to the forefront of these debates, rather than effectiveness in reducing criminal activity.

Examiner tip
Practise 'real' exam questions as often as you can. Look at the answers in this unit guide and use them as exemplars to help you improve your own performance.

Synoptic links

To methodological issues

Studies of criminal justice tend to rely on secondary sources, such as court reports or media accounts of events, because it is, for example, difficult to gain first-hand experience of prisons.

Subjectivity This occurs when personal opinions and beliefs interfere in the knowledge-creating process, so that bias occurs.

To other areas of the course

The Marxist approach argues for a clear correspondence between factories and prisons, while Foucauldians argue that the routines of the prison are diffusing throughout the rest of society in a seamless web of power.

To theoretical issues

Debates about these issues often take place at a level of high abstraction and principles, so that there is always a danger of subjectivity entering into the debate.

Key concepts

new punitiveness, correspondence, risk society, incarceration, incapacitation theory, actuarial justice, technology of governance, respect agenda

Key thinkers

Ericson, Melossi and Pavarini, Spierenburg, Cohen, Rusche and Kirchheimer, Moore, Lee

Victims

Key ideas

- The issue of the victims of crime has become a central aspect of the sociology of crime as society's concern has moved away from dealing with offenders to compensating victims.
- Victims have a formal role to play in criminal proceedings, rights to compensation being established in law and police 'counting rules' taking the victim's perspective into consideration.
- There are debates among sociologists about a typology of victimhood, with some controversy about whether there is such a thing as a provoking victim.
- People can be victims of corporate and state crimes, not just at the mercy of individual criminals.
- An important aspect of victimology is the 'fear of crime' debate in which we place ourselves potentially as victims in an imagined state of being victimised by high levels of crime.
- An industry of security devices has been constructed around our fears of being a victim.
- Women are more likely to be victims of crime than men and British ethnic minority individuals are proportionately more likely to be victimised than whites.

Typology A way of organising and categorising something by reference to similarities and differences, which makes it easier to understand and explore.

Knowledge check 23

Give an example of a security device that an individual may use.

- Gay men are more likely to be victimised than straight men because they suffer from homophobic attacks.
- Many female victims remain invisible because much violence (sexual and physical) is acquaintance abuse — that is, perpetrated by someone close to them.
- Restorative justice programmes seek to bring offender and victim together, so that resolution and compensation can be established between them.

Evaluation

+ The focus on the victim restores a sense of balance in the criminal justice system, which some would argue has tilted too far towards the rights of the criminal.

+ Research into victims has led to policies of support for victims and strategies for reducing the risk of becoming a victim.

+ Discovering the extent of victimisation in the home has moved debates about crime off the street and back into the family.

– The emphasis on victims has created a culture in which everyone is looking to complain and gain compensation.

– Victimology focuses mainly on the relationship between individual offenders and victims and ignores wider victimisation by corporations and states.

– Restorative justice programmes are not systematic enough to make a difference to most victims and they do not always lead to a satisfactory outcome for victims.

Examiner tip

Organise your revision so that you are not doing everything at the last minute — you need to get a good night's sleep before the exam.

Synoptic links

To methodological issues

It is difficult to develop a research instrument that would consistently capture the emotion of the 'fear of crime' because it means many different things to different people and it is impossible to measure the intensity of that fear in a scientific way.

To other areas of the course

Issues of gender, ethnicity and locality are central to an understanding of victims. Therefore, links to stratification and differentiation can be made. In addition, the number of victims of **domestic violence** suggests that the 'dark side' of the family could be connected to victimology.

To theoretical issues

Feminism draws attention to the fact that many women are victims of criminal actions by men and links this to the patriarchal nature of society in which the wishes and desires of men are paramount.

Domestic violence Physical or psychological harm carried out in the home usually, but not exclusively, by men on women.

Key concepts

restorative justice, global victimology, fear of crime, culture of complaint, provoking victims, willing victims, acquaintance crime

Key thinkers

Mendelsohn, Quinney, Tombs and Williams, Hughes, Fattah, Goodey

Summary

- The activities of the police and other law enforcement agencies are as important as the activities of criminals.
- The legal framework of a society provides the context for the study of crime and is open to political and social manipulation.
- The workings of the criminal justice system and the role of prisons are highly politicised and swing between punishment and rehabilitation.
- Victims are increasingly studied as part of the sociology of crime and deviance as well as a focus for restorative justice schemes.

The sociological study of suicide

Durkheimian tradition and suicide

Key ideas

- That the most individual of all acts, the taking of one's own life, is subject to social influences, which have a real existence beyond the individual.
- Suicide is defined as any action or inaction that directly or indirectly leads to the individual taking his or her own life.
- Durkheim rejected both biological (hereditary) and psychological explanations of the suicide rate.
- While accepting that some individuals were more prone to suicidal acts than others, the force that determines the rate of suicide is social and related to the amount of integration or regulation in society.
- Too much or too little regulation and too much or too little integration lead to different forms of suicide.
- Later Durkheimians relate suicide rate to the stability of social relationships in society, with lower status integration leading to higher suicide rates.
- Refinements of Durkheim's theories tend to simplify the four-fold division of suicide because of the difficulty in separating out altruistic, fatalistic, egoistic and anomic acts.

Knowledge check 24

Give an example of how inaction may lead to a person's suicide.

Integration Social processes that bind an individual to society as a whole.

Evaluation

+ Established a specifically sociological view of the individual.

+ Explains different suicide rates in different countries by reference to their social characteristics.

+ Emphasises the power of social forces in shaping individual lives.

− Denies the importance of individual choice in the act of suicide.

− Does not explain why suicidogenic impulses are translated into suicide in some predisposed individuals and not others.

− Suicide statistics are themselves open to question about their validity.

Examiner tip

In the exam, divide your time appropriately for the number of marks and make sure that you attempt all the questions you are required to.

Synoptic links

To methodological issues

The use of official statistics as a basis for explaining the incidence of suicide in different societies has been subject to a great deal of methodological scrutiny with the conclusion that, while they do seem to show **patterned regularities** with remarkable consistency, they are subject to social construction processes.

Patterned regularities Statistical features of society that exhibit enduring similarities across time and space, with limited variation

To other areas of the course

Durkheim's starting point was the 'problem of order' — how do individuals with all their selfishness manage to live together in society? This is one of the fundamental questions in any discussion of power and politics.

To theoretical issues

Durkheim's insistence on the real existence of social forces has provoked much debate, with interactionists in particular seeing this as a reification of society.

Key concepts

regulation, integration, suicidogenic impulse, altruistic, anomic, fatalistic, egoistic, reification

Key thinkers

Durkheim, Gibbs and Martin, Ginsberg

Ecological approaches

Key ideas

- Developed out of the Chicago School tradition, this approach argues that there is an 'urban trend' in the suicide rate, with cities showing consistently greater incidence of suicide than rural areas.
- Comparing different areas of the city shows consistently high levels of suicide in localities with the characteristics of social disorganisation.
- Indicators such as high levels of rented accommodation, divorce and pawn shops are related to high levels of suicide.
- Inner-city areas have concentrations of individuals with the highest level of personal disorganisation who are more likely to seek to take their own lives.
- It is, therefore, not poverty that, of itself, leads people to commit suicide in these areas. It is the mobility and lack of social cohesion and community, which might make those who could withstand disruption within a strong community turn to suicide as a way out.
- Unemployment is a factor, because becoming unemployed also means the individual is cut off from the work community and the resources that enable individuals to participate fully in communal life.

Knowledge check 25

Why are pawn shops an indicator of social disorganisation?

Evaluation

+ This approach focuses on the nature of community life as an explanation for differential suicide rates.

+ Recognises the importance of economic factors in explaining high rates of suicide and includes unemployment as a factor.

+ Involves an element of social change in its theory, in insisting upon rate of growth, rather than just size, as the important dimension.

− There is a danger of an ecological fallacy — that is, the inadmissibility of reading from the general characteristics of a population as a whole (all those in an area) to a constituent group within it (those who commit suicide).

− It is not made clear how the social disorganisation of an area is related to individual decisions to commit suicide.

− It takes the suicide statistics at face value, when they are in fact problematic.

Examiner tip

Carry out a 'question audit' before you begin your answer so that you know exactly what skills are being requested and on what issues.

Synoptic links

To methodological issues

This approach employs the classical sociological method of comparison, in this case between rural and urban areas and the suicide rates within them. Cavan, for example, compared the official statistics (including suicide) for 72 areas of Chicago to arrive at her conclusions.

To other areas of the course

This approach can be related in part to the area of the sociology of work, where sociologists are interested in the effect of unemployment on the unemployed.

To theoretical issues

This is a classical **positivistic** approach to an issue, relying on the official statistics to represent a real social phenomenon accurately. Anti-positivists would be critical of such an approach for ignoring individual motivations in committing a suicidal act.

Positivism An approach to sociology that attempts to be as close to the natural sciences as possible.

Key concepts

urban trend, community, social disorganisation, personal disorganisation, ecological fallacy

Key thinkers

Cavan, Sainsbury, Weschler

Interactionist approaches

Key ideas

- The official statistics on suicide are the product of social construction through the actions of a large number of people.
- Deaths are not always easy to characterise as accidental, suicidal, natural or murder and thus there is space for interpretation of an individual death by social agencies.
- Even to characterise a death as 'suspicious' is open to interpretation, with different social actors likely to view the same events in a different way.
- A crucial actor in the decision to define a death as suicide is the coroner and coroners employ different 'rules of thumb' when making their decisions. Some sociologists, therefore, argue that we should reject suicide statistics as unreliable. Others suggest that we should be sceptical about them, and still others argue for a limited acceptance of them as rough indicators of suicide rates.
- Moral factors intrude on the decision of key actors to define a death as a suicide or not, with, for example, Catholics being more reluctant to 'stigmatise' a death as suicide because of its sinful implications.
- Therefore, suicide does not exist beyond the meaning that we, as **social actors**, give to it.

Knowledge check 26

Which social agencies are likely to be involved in the characterisation of a death?

Social actors Individuals carrying out their lives in relation to other individuals and the institutions that they inhabit.

Evaluation

+ Draws attention to the important social processes underlying the creation of suicide statistics.

+ Emphasises the ambiguity of all social actions, even seemingly obvious ones like dying.

+ Introduces the moral dimension into the sociological consideration of suicidal actions.

– The suicide statistics of a country do show remarkable stability across time, despite the large number of individual decisions that have to be made to compile them.

– Any errors in the suicide statistics are random rather than systematic and, therefore, to an extent, they can be relied on.

– By rejecting statistics, the opportunities to discuss trends over time and comparisons between countries are removed.

Examiner tip

Make sure that you write in good English in the examination, checking your work if you have time.

Synoptic links

To methodological issues

The critique of the official suicide statistics is an exemplary case for dealing with all official statistics, no matter how hard or soft. The key limitation of the official statistics is that they do not establish the intention of the individual who is said to have committed suicide.

To other areas of the course

Postmodernism An approach within sociology that suggests that no knowledge is certain.

The role of the doctor in defining particular acts as suicide — natural or suspicious — focuses our attention on the power of the medical profession and the medical gaze in **postmodern** societies.

To theoretical issues

The interactionist emphasis on the meanings that individuals attach to a particular social action is central to action theory, delineating it from more structural theories such as functionalism and Marxism.

Key concepts

social construction, coroners' definitions, soft statistics, suicidal acts

Key thinkers

Cicourel, Taylor, Douglas, Atkinson

Contemporary approaches

Key ideas

- Attempted suicides are not just failed suicides, but represent a different level of meaning for actions aimed at suicide.
- The meanings that can be attached to suicidal acts are much more varied than someone attempting to kill himself or herself.
- Attempted or failed suicidal acts have social consequences involving support agencies, family, peers and work.
- It is often difficult to distinguish between those actions that are genuine attempts to end one's life, and those that are a cry for help.
- Many suicidal actions are 'gambles with death', in which the outcome of the action is uncertain and determined by factors out of the control of the 'suicide', such as chance discovery. They are, therefore, aimed at life and death at the same time.
- However, the actor can influence the outcome through the method of suicide chosen, the location, and the events leading up to and including the process of dying itself.
- Intentions can be inferred, but not completely known, through an examination of all the contingent circumstances surrounding the suicidal act.

Meanings (behind actions) These are an important element in understanding actions and refer to the intention(s) of the individual carrying out the action.

Knowledge check 27

What is one of the main ways that sociologists can access the intentions of a suicide?

Evaluation

+ Provides a more complex understanding of the nature and potential outcomes of suicidal acts.

+ Places the act of suicide into the social, as well as personal, circumstances surrounding it.

+ Refers to the consequences of the suicidal action and not just causes.

− It is difficult to discuss trends in rates of suicide, given the uncertainty of outcome at the heart of these approaches.

− It compels the sociologist of suicide to examine each situation individually, with a resultant difficulty in drawing generalisations.

− Even a consideration of all circumstances leaves an element of the unknown in terms of intention.

Examiner tip
Read any items of information attached to a question carefully — they will help you to focus on the issue raised.

Synoptic links

To methodological issues

The problem of finding a method of accessing another's intentions is highlighted in these approaches. While the motivation for the suicide act may be expressed by the suicide themselves (to friends, in notes etc.), whether the real intention was to die or to be discovered has to be gleaned from an examination of the circumstances in which the act takes place.

Legal constraints The ways in which the law defines activities as either lawful or unlawful, and thus shapes the actions of individuals in society.

To other areas of the course

The issue of suicide can be linked to both the sociology of law, in that it has been subject to different legal constraints over the years, and to the issues of health and welfare, as the agencies that have to deal with the aftermath of a suicide attempt will include medical, psychological and social services.

To theoretical issues

The focus on inferring intentions provides a link to Weberian approaches to social life. Being adequate at the level of meaning is a central tenet of Weber's approach.

Key concepts

attempted suicide, gambles with death, contingent factors, intentions

Key thinkers

Stengel, Taylor, Weiss

Summary

- The study of suicide is at the heart of the original sociological enterprise.
- Patterns of suicide between countries and localities have been central to an understanding of the causes of suicide.
- The meaning attached to suicidal acts is important in understanding the seriousness of any individual act.
- Suicidal acts are not easily categorised as certain, gambles with death or cries for help.

Questions & Answers

How to use this section

This section of the guide provides you with sample questions on the topic of **Crime and Deviance** in the style of the AQA Unit 4 test. There are two types of question. Questions 01 and 02 focus just on crime and deviance. Question 03 is a Methods in Context question which asks you to apply your understanding of research methods to a particular aspect of crime and deviance.

Two examples of questions 01 and 02 are provided. Each is followed by both an A-grade and a C-grade student response. You should note that the A-grade responses are not 'model' answers and represent only one way in which the questions might be answered. You can use other material, adopt a different approach, make different synoptic links and come to a different conclusion and still obtain good marks. However, the answers do show you how to approach these sorts of questions.

The first Methods in Context question 03 also has a C-grade and an A-grade answer. The second (03) Methods in Context question is provided at the end for you to try by yourself without the support of a student answer. Some guidance is given to help you answer it correctly.

Like all responses in AS and A2, the student answers the question set, and not one that they would like to answer. The response demonstrates the skills that are required in the specification, including good written communication skills of spelling, punctuation and grammar. Therefore, the best answers are critical and evaluative, use concepts appropriately and have a sound structure. The C-grade answers show a student who is on the right track, but who has made some errors that mean the response cannot obtain the highest marks.

Examiner's comments

Examiner comments are provided for each question. These give tips on what you need to do to gain full marks and are indicated by the ⓔ icon.

The student's answers are interspersed with examiner's comments, preceded by the ⓔ icon. These comments identify why high marks have been given and where improvements might be made, especially in the C grade responses. You may wish to rewrite the C-grade answers to see if you can improve on the performance, using the advice given.

Examinable skills

A2 Sociology papers are designed to test certain defined skills. These skills are expressed as assessment objectives in the specification. You will have already been tested on these assessment objectives in your AS Sociology examinations, but the weighting for each of the two assessment objectives (AO1 and AO2) is different for the A2 Sociology specification. Over the two units of A2, the proportion of marks given to AO1 (Knowledge and Understanding) is just over 40% and for AO2 (Application, Analysis, Interpretation and Evaluation) is just under 60%. The effect of this is that you have to be able to demonstrate more sophisticated skills of analysis and evaluation at A2 than at AS. You will be required to show a more critical, reflective and evaluative approach to methodological issues, to the nature of sociological enquiry and to sociological debates, based on a broad and diverse range of sources.

In addition, Unit 4, of which Crime and Deviance is one of the options, carries slightly more weight (30% of the whole A-level) in the A2 part of the examination than Unit 3 (20%). Both units assess the synoptic element of the A-level course. Synoptic assessment is defined as the drawing together of knowledge, understanding and skills learned in different aspects of the course. This means that you will have to make connections to other topics you have studied at both AS and A2, including the core themes. You are also required to link, where appropriate, your study of crime and deviance to issues concerning the nature of sociological thought that are identified in AO1 and to methods of sociological enquiry. In addition, Unit 4 students are encouraged to draw upon any small-scale research they have carried out themselves and, in question 03, are required explicitly to apply knowledge of research methods to an issue within crime and deviance.

Assessment objective 1 (AO1)

AO1 concerns the paired skills of **knowledge and understanding**. You have to demonstrate clearly to the examiners that you have appropriate, accurate *knowledge* and a good *understanding* of the sociological material in the topic you are studying. The Content guidance section provided an account of the basic knowledge needed in crime and deviance. The reason for bringing together knowledge and understanding is that in the examination, it is not enough to be able to reproduce knowledge learned by rote. You must also be able to use it in a meaningful way to answer the specific question set. This includes the ability to select the most appropriate information from the range of knowledge that you have. This is particularly important in synoptic assessment, as the whole of the course can be drawn upon to show your command of the connections between different parts of the course. In addition, you have to demonstrate your knowledge and understanding of the core themes of the specification. These are:

- socialisation, culture and identity
- social differentiation, power and stratification

Aspects of these themes are dealt with in various elements of the AS and A2 courses. Therefore, the themes run through the whole of the course and that includes the topic of crime and deviance. Examples of where these are dealt with are included in the Content guidance section as well as in this section. However, you will also be able to make links to these themes through your consideration of the relationship between crime and deviance and other substantive topics, such as the Family and Households or Beliefs in Society.

One of the demands of synoptic assessment is that you make connections between sociological methods and crime and deviance and this is directly assessed in question 03 of the examination. The specification requires that you have a good knowledge and understanding of a range of sociological methods and sources, and that, in particular, you understand the relationship between theory and methods. This includes the ways that sociologists:

- acquire primary and secondary data
- analyse qualitative and quantitative data using appropriate concepts
- design and execute sociological research
- are influenced by theoretical, practical and ethical considerations in their research

The nature of sociological thought is concerned with both concepts and sociological theories. A requirement of synoptic assessment is that you make the links between these concepts and theories and the substantive area you have chosen to study — in this case, crime and deviance. The nature of sociological thought covers:

- social order and social control
- social change
- conflict and consensus
- social structure and social action
- the role of values
- the relationship between sociology and contemporary social policy

Part of the AO1 skills concerns the quality of written communication and includes the ability to:

- use a style of writing appropriate for transmitting complex information
- organise information coherently, using specialist vocabulary such as sociological concepts when appropriate
- use accurate spelling, punctuation and grammar to ensure that the meaning is clear and the text is legible

Assessment objective 2 (AO2)

AO2 covers **application**, **analysis**, **interpretation and evaluation**. At A2, more marks are given to AO2 skills than to AO1 skills, so you will need to be more critical and evaluative than in the AS exams. You will therefore need to:

- select and apply appropriate pieces of sociological knowledge and arguments and distinguish between facts and opinion (**application**)
- break down sociological studies and debates into their component parts, such as concepts, perspectives, methods, findings, conclusions, strengths and weaknesses (**analysis**)
- examine material such as text, statistics, tables, graphs and research findings to identify trends and establish their meaning and importance (**interpretation**)
- assess the relevance and importance of sociological studies and debates, conveying their strengths and weaknesses and coming to a conclusion about them (**evaluation**)

Evaluation is a particularly important skill at A2, and for every piece of sociological research or approach that you come across you should be constantly asking the questions: 'Why should I believe this?', 'What evidence is there for this viewpoint?', 'Are there any counter-arguments?' and 'Who says so?'. Try to develop the habit of evaluation as you progress through your course. A good way to do this is to establish a minimum of two strengths and two weaknesses for every piece of research or every point of view or sociological perspective that you examine. Even better, try to come to a conclusion about whether it/they are convincing or not, with your conclusion backed by rational argument and solid sociological research.

Part of the AO2 skills includes the ability to:
- organise your arguments coherently
- display an understanding of theoretical debates in sociology
- marshal evidence to support arguments and any conclusions you make

The unit test

The paper

Crime and Deviance is a Unit 4 topic. Unit 4 also contains the topic Stratification and Differentiation. It is unlikely that you will have covered both Crime and Deviance and Stratification and Differentiation in your course, but, if you have, you must choose only one of the two sections on the examination paper. In the Crime and Deviance section, the first two questions (01 and 02) are concerned with crime and deviance. Question 03 is a Methods in Context question where you have to apply your understanding of sociological methods to a particular aspect of crime and deviance. In addition, you have to answer a freestanding question (question 04 in the Crime and Deviance section, question 08 in the Stratification and Differentiation section) on theory and methods.

You have to answer all four questions in each section. Therefore, having chosen the Crime and Deviance section, you have no choices left — you must answer all questions in that section. These questions are worth 30% of the whole A-level qualification and are therefore an important component. The Crime and Deviance section is worth 90 marks in total.

Question structure

- Questions 01 and 02 are on any aspect of crime and deviance and are worth 21 marks each.
- Question 03 has a methodological focus, in that you will be required to apply a research method or methods to the study of a specific issue in crime and deviance.

Attached to each of the first three questions will be a single **Item** of source material (Item A for question 01, Item B for question 02 and Item C for question 03). These are designed to help you by providing information from which you may draw to answer the questions set. You should always read this material carefully first, before attempting to answer the question. It may provide you with important clues to answering it. The questions refer specifically to the Item ('With reference to Item A' or 'Using Item A and evidence from any part of the course'), so you are **required** to make use of the source material. You should do this as obviously as possible to assist the marker in identifying where in your answer you have obeyed the instruction. For example, you might write, 'As Item A demonstrates...' or 'The view in Item A suggests a functionalist approach is most useful...'

The division of marks between the questions (21 for question 01, 21 for question 02, 15 for question 03 and 33 for question 04) indicates the time that you should allocate to each part. As you have 2 hours, you should take note of the advice on the front page of the paper and spend approximately 30 minutes on question 01, 30 minutes on question 02, 20 minutes on question 03 and 40 minutes on question 04. The balance of AO1 and AO2 marks in all four questions is weighted towards AO2 skills. For question 01, AO1 is given 9 marks and AO2 12 marks. The same distribution is given in question 02. For question 03, AO1 is given 6 marks and AO2 9 marks. The important thing to remember is that the skills of **application, analysis, interpretation and evaluation** are the most important in A2 examinations and therefore you must ensure that you demonstrate them. Pay particular attention to the wording of questions, which provides you with clues as to the particular skills being asked for. Note, however, that you need to provide evidence of knowledge and understanding of material from crime and deviance in both question 01 and question 02, so you should not neglect this skill either.

You should note that both question 01 and question 02 are given 21 marks, with the balance tipped towards AO2 (12 against 9 for AO1).

Question 03 is the innovative feature of Unit 4. The question requires you to apply your knowledge and understanding of the way sociologists go about their research to a particular issue in crime and deviance. The particular issue will be identified for you in the Item — Item C (which is why it is essential that you read it) — and the question will identify the research method(s) that you have to apply.

This does *not* mean that you have to know about specific sociological studies of crime and deviance that have used the method being examined. Rather, you have to employ your sociological imagination to explore the strengths and weaknesses of particular methods in studying a specific issue, such as, for example, girl gangs. However, there are certain questions that you might ask of yourself to help you apply your sociological imagination:

(1) What are the characteristics of the group being studied that might make it easy or difficult to use the identified method?

(2) What are the characteristics of the researcher that might make it easy or difficult to use the identified method?

(3) What is the context/background of the group being studied that might make it easy or difficult to use the identified method?

(4) What are the strengths and weaknesses of the identified method that might make it easy or difficult to research this particular issue?

For example, in the case of girl gangs, a male researcher might have difficulty in gaining access to the gang if he was employing an observational method. If the members of the girl gang are engaging in criminal behaviour, then they might resist being observed at all or not be honest in responding in an interview, and so on.

To see the range of issues that may be examined in crime and deviance, refer back to the Content guidance section of this guide.

Example I

Question 01 Deviancy amplification

Read Item A and answer the question that follows.

Item A

The concepts of the folk devil and moral panic were first developed in Stanley Cohen's study of the 'mods and rockers' of the 1960s. These subcultural groups were involved in some minor public disorder events one bank holiday in the seaside town of Clacton. The newspapers sensationalised these events, splashing them across their front pages. Their exaggerated reports created public fear and a hostile reaction to the youth groups, which were seen as a major threat to public order. Mod and rocker subcultures received publicity, which led more teenagers to adopt these styles, further increasing public fear in a deviancy amplification spiral. Mods and rockers became what Cohen called the 'folk devils' of their time.

(01) **Using information from Item A and elsewhere, evaluate the importance of the mass media in the amplification of deviance.**

(21 marks)

ⓔ The question is asking you to evaluate. Therefore you must consider the weaknesses as well as the strengths of the view that links the media to the amplification of deviance. You need to be clear in your understanding of what amplification entails and the traditional way that the mass media have been connected to that process. Remember, however, that there may be more than one way in which the mass media are involved in amplification and that other social agents may also be involved. It may be that considering alternative agents of amplification will impact on how far you conclude that it is the media that are most important in amplification.

C-grade answer

The role of the mass media in the amplification of deviance has been a concern of sociologists for some time. From the 1960s, when Cohen studied the mods and rockers until today, with dole scroungers **a**. The term amplification means something getting worse and here it refers to the ways in which newspaper reports can make an undesirable event worse. The work of Cohen on amplification suggested that the media's exaggeration of violence resulted in more violence actually being committed **b**.

ⓔ **a** Note that the second 'sentence' is actually not a full sentence. Remember that the quality of written work is also taken into account and you should be careful to write in full sentences at all times when writing essays. **b** There is a fairly good, if basic, account of Cohen's views in this paragraph, although the last point made is open to different interpretations. Do you agree that 'amplification' means 'getting worse'?

There are various stages in the amplification of deviance. The first is where a group or an individual commits an antisocial action, such as a football hooligan. This is picked up by the media, which report it to the public. Because of sensationalism **c**, the public becomes concerned about the group and asks for more laws to deal with the problem. Politicians **d** respond because they want to be popular. As a result of this process, a moral panic has been created about a folk devil.

ⓔ **c** The description of the process could be much more firmly focused on the role of the media. For example, the student refers to sensationalism, but not in the context of the media. For example, how do the media sensationalise and why do they do it? To score marks, the connections to other areas of study should be explicitly made. **d** This could also be done when the student writes about politicians. Similarly, the student applies appropriate concepts (moral panic and folk devil) but does not make connections to the media — for example, to the selection and presentation of media content, media representations etc.

The media create folk devils **e** through misrepresenting them in their reports. They produce accounts of people that make them appear a lot worse than they actually are. This is called stereotyping and journalists are responsible for doing this to certain social groups **f**. Sometimes this involves the media in victim blaming, in that some vulnerable groups like asylum seekers are shown as frauds **g**, when they may really be oppressed in their home country.

ⓔ **c** This paragraph has some potential, because it is seeking to apply some concepts to the issue of amplification and is focused on the role of the media. **f** For example, stereotyping is deployed effectively here. **g** Victim blaming is also used and is supported by an example. However, victim blaming could have been better explained than it is.

The media are not all bad. They do give us our knowledge of the world and without them we would not have such a great understanding of social events **h** The media are in competition with each other and there is a tendency to over-emphasise things which will sell newspapers. Nevertheless they do report real events, even if not always fully or with slight exaggerations.

ⓔ **h** This paragraph is attempting to show that the media are not just about creating folk devils but have some positive aspects also. As such, there is an evaluative edge to it, but it should be more clearly focused on the question set.

The process of deviancy amplification has been criticised by some sociologists. It is argued that the process is presented in a sort of automatic way in which the public responds to media reports, when sociologists such as McRobbie suggest that there are more complicated forces at work. For example, folk devil styles are often taken up by the fashion or culture industry and promoted as an alternative lifestyle rather than a deviant subculture. This idea is linked to the sociology of culture **i**.

ⓔ **i** There is an explicit link in this last sentence to the sociology of culture. Not only does this paragraph gain AO2 marks, but it also fulfils the requirement that connections are made to other areas of the course, through the reference to the core theme of culture.

The media are clearly involved in the process of deviancy amplification, among other things they do. By showing social groups in a particular light, it provokes a reaction from others, and this is demonstrated by many studies in this area, such as Fishman's **j**. This leads to more control over the folk devil group and also changes to the way in which the folk devils perceive themselves and behave. The end result is an increase in the originally reported deviance.

ⓔ **j** As a conclusion, this contains some new information that would have been better contained in the main body of the answer. Nevertheless, it does score marks for knowledge and understanding. The student has taken a particular position on the evaluation of the process and supported it with reference to empirical material. A more sophisticated view of the processes involved would have been rewarded even higher. In all, the answer would score 6 marks for AO1 and 4 marks for AO2.

ⓔ **Overall mark: 10/21**

A-grade answer

To answer this question fully, we must draw upon sociological understandings of the mass media as well as deviance **a**. The idea of deviancy amplification is firmly within the interactionist tradition **b** and comes out of a consideration of the processes of labelling and self-fulfilling prophecy, which are important in the sociological study of deviance and education **c**. Cohen developed the idea of the amplification of deviance spiral from his interest in the contradiction that the media often raged against deviant or criminal behaviour, but in so doing, often made the 'problem' worse. He was interested in the process whereby the media contributed to an increase in the very behaviour they were criticising.

ⓔ **a** The opening sentence immediately recognises the demands of the question. It signals to the examiner that the student has made the link to another substantive topic in sociology. **b** The answer also makes a theoretical link, which, though not a requirement of the question itself, does show that the student has a good understanding of the whole of sociology. **c** This is reinforced by the connection made through labelling to the area of education.

Cohen's work was concerned with the mods and rockers and some incidents on the seafront one bank holiday. Although the original incidents were relatively minor — some scuffling and shoving and a lot of drunkenness — the papers chose to headline **d** the violence as if it was much worse than it was. Cohen established this through content analysis **e** of the newspapers. This kind of reporting created concern among the readers, the police and moral entrepreneurs in society and led to demands that something must be done about 'the young people of today'. Thus, concern is described by interactionists as a 'moral panic' about whoever is the 'folk devil' of the day. The media create folk devils all the time. The mods and rockers were in the 1960s, but today we might have asylum seekers or teenagers with knives. It does not even have to be an identifiable group. The European Union is presented as a folk devil by some papers **f**.

ⓔ This paragraph is descriptive of Cohen's work and as 9 of the 21 marks available are for AO1 (knowledge and understanding), this is a good tactic by the student. There are also some AO2 marks to be awarded here, especially because he or she is also showing synoptic links. **d** For example, look at the way that the student introduces the concept of headlining, which is normally associated with the study of the sociology of the media. **e** There is a link to methodology made through content analysis. **f** The paragraph also shows some good application skills in the use of examples — moving from the 1960s to contemporary society.

The effects of being labelled as a folk devil by the media are two-fold. First, it changes the way that the police and the courts deal with the social group involved. For example, there was a greater police presence on the seafront at the next bank holiday, with the result that more mods and rockers were caught doing violent things and so the problem seemed to be getting worse. It might mean, however, that no more violence was occurring, but the same level was noticed more. The second effect is that it changes the way the mods and rockers see themselves, so that they begin to take on the 'master status' **g** of folk devil and act out their roles as the media have defined them. This is why it is often called a social reaction theory **h**.

ⓔ **g** Again, there is a good use of concepts here, for example, master status. The focus of this paragraph is still description, but it draws upon deviance and media equally. **h** Understanding is also shown by the correct use of 'social reaction theory'

There is some dispute about the implications of amplification among sociologists. Some argue that the media do actually create more deviance through their reporting **i**, while others argue that the incidence of deviance does not increase, it is just the sensational reporting of the press that makes it look like there is an increase **j**. It may be that there are different effects for different folk devils **k**. For example, more young people might become mods and rockers when they read about it or see them on the television. Alexander argues that in the case of satanic abuse, there would not be a great rush to join such folk devil groups.

ⓔ There is quite a sophisticated debate going on here and it demonstrates some good AO2 skills by the student. **i j** The paragraph presents two sides of a sociological argument, **k** but then shows that social life is much more complicated than a black and white debate would suggest.

The idea of a deviancy amplification spiral has found much support **l** from empirical studies of the media and deviant groups — for example, smokers of marijuana. The process is one that strikes a chord among many people as an obvious way in which the media construct concern among the public by choosing to emphasise and sensationalise particular events. However, it is also clear that the process cannot

be as automatic as it is sometimes presented **m**. The media are actually made up of a large number of gatekeepers, who control access to the making of the news and who are unlikely all to follow the same stories. Indeed, many newspapers are rivals and take different stands on issues to demonstrate their difference. So, they do not always turn the same 'gaze' upon a group or event.

Another problem with the media side of the process is that it tends to assume that the audience **n** for the media reports all receive exactly the same message from the media. Yet, implicit in the account is the idea that there are at least two different reactions to the media accounts — the one from moral entrepreneurs **o** and the public and the other from the folk devils themselves. Why should there just be two ways in which the media message can be interpreted?

(e) **l** We begin here to stack up some AO2 points and **m** are moving towards evaluation. **o** There are some sophisticated points made in this paragraph and some inventive use of concepts. Look at the way that the student uses 'gaze' to describe what the media do. This idea is usually connected to the sociology of medicine or the professions, so its use here is further evidence of the student drawing on material from the whole of the course. **n** The argument presented about the audience is well made and represents sophisticated application and assessment skills. Material from the topic of the mass media is used well and applied to the question.

So, to conclude, it may be **p** that the media are an important avenue for the creation of folk devils and moral panics, but it is not a straightforward road. The media are not an undifferentiated agency and people do not respond to them in a deterministic way. People can use media reports for their own purposes — they can even manipulate the media to create an image that they desire. It is also not clear that our understanding of society can be separated from the media who are our prime source of information **q**. Yet, certain social groups do come to be seen as undesirable or a problem in society and as we get our information about them from the media rather than first hand, then it is likely that the media do play a significant role in the process of deviancy amplification.

(e) This comes to a good conclusion. **p** Note that it does not really come down on one side or the other. This is fine, especially as we are dealing with a complex process here. **q** What the paragraph does do is lay out both sides of the debate and alert the reader to the complex and unfinished nature of this debate. Clearly, we have a very good answer here. It is both knowledgeable and skilful. There are some issues that might have been included and some other pros and cons to be discussed. In the time available, this does an excellent job of covering the issue and scores 8 for AO1 and 11 for AO2.

(e) **Overall mark: 19/21**

Question 02 **Ethnic minorities and crime**

Read Item B and answer the question that follows.

Item B

There are two main ideas about the apparent over-representation of ethnic minorities in the criminal statistics. The first accepts that there is some reality to the frequency with which the ethnic minorities appear in the statistics and therefore the task is to explain why ethnic minorities are more 'criminal'. The second suggests that the statistics exaggerate ethnic minority criminal behaviour and therefore the task is to explain the social processes that ensure the ethnic minorities are over-represented in them. There is a third position that puts forward the idea that to lump all ethnic minorities together is to misrepresent the relationship between different social groups and criminal activity.

(02) Using material from Item B and elsewhere, evaluate how far official statistics present a valid picture of the criminal activities of ethnic minorities.

(21 marks)

(e) To answer this question, you need to know accurately what is meant by 'valid'. The question is asking if the official statistics of crime represent the 'real' rate and patterns of offending, in relation to ethnic minorities. You must be careful to focus on this social group and sociological work that looks at ethnic minorities in relation to crime when choosing which studies and arguments to include in your answer. You should try to avoid sociological work that is about official statistics generally, unless you specifically and relevantly apply such work to the circumstances of ethnic minorities.

C-grade answer

The official statistics of crime and ethnicity do in the main provide a valid view of the criminal activity of ethnic minorities **a**, although there are some problems with their collection and recording. The explanations that sociologists have put forward to account for the higher levels of crime among black young men vary according to perspective and willingness to accept the official statistics as real **b**.

(e) **a** The answer starts with a strong statement about the relationship between the statistics and ethnicity, and in one sense tries to answer the question before any discussion. **b** However, there is a qualification included at the end of the first sentence and at the end of the paragraph, which might allow some late focus on the methodological issue.

Traditional explanations on ethnicity focused on the areas in which black people lived as an explanation for engaging more in crime. They looked at the social disorganisation of inner city areas and concluded that it was the lack of community integration and the existence of weak social networks that led members of minority

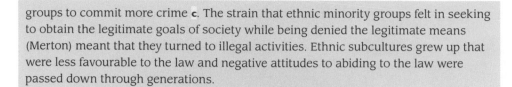

groups to commit more crime **c**. The strain that ethnic minority groups felt in seeking to obtain the legitimate goals of society while being denied the legitimate means (Merton) meant that they turned to illegal activities. Ethnic subcultures grew up that were less favourable to the law and negative attitudes to abiding to the law were passed down through generations.

🄴 **c** The paragraph offers an overview of sociocultural explanations of ethnicity and crime, including reference to Merton (interpretation skill). It would have been better if the student had explicitly described the traditional explanations' acceptance of the statistics as real, rather than just take it for granted. A direct reference to the Item would have helped here.

Left realists argue that black people commit more crime because they are marginalised in society, through housing, lack of economic opportunity, and a loss of traditional masculine identity **d**. They turn to illegal activities such as selling drugs, therefore, as a means of income support and also as a means of gaining status in their peer group. Because black youngsters experience prejudice and discrimination in society, they become frustrated and turn to violence to express this (Sellin).

🄴 **d** Again, there is a fair description of the realist approach, but there is little explicit reference to the wider dimension of the question. The student is making some synoptic links to theories, but the question requires discussion of how realists view and use official statistics in relation to ethnic minority crime.

Social construction approaches argue that the official statistics are not real but are socially constructed through the activities of the police **e**. Therefore by choosing to patrol certain areas of the city rather than others, the police ensure that there are more members of ethnic minorities caught. Once caught, it is more likely that black as opposed to white men will proceed to trial, with white offenders gaining more cautions. In court, black people are more likely to be given a custodial sentence. This shows that it is not the case that black people commit more crime than white people, but that they are more likely to appear in the official statistics of crime because of the way that the criminal justice system operates **f**.

🄴 **e** This is more focused, because the student is using the social construction approach to explore the relationship between the official statistics of crime and ethnicity. **f** Some good evaluation points are made as the processes of law enforcement are described.

Critical criminologists **g** argue that it is part of the ideological and economic processes of capitalism to divide white from black workers and treat blacks as a reserve army of labour. This means that they are more likely to be made unemployed in times of difficulties and to turn to crime to make ends meet. Black people are defined as the 'Other' and seen as more likely to be criminal than the law-abiding host community. This is known as the new racism.

🅔 **g** Another theoretical approach is described here, making a link to theory but not directly addressing the issue of official statistics. More effective use of the Item would have helped the student to keep focused on the issue of statistics.

> The way the relationship between official statistics and ethnic minorities is viewed therefore depends on the perspective adopted. Different sociologists explain the appearance of blacks in the crime statistics in different ways and one of those ways is the biased view of the official statistics.

🅔 The conclusion seems at odds with the opening sentence of the answer. The student has tried to tell a story about ethnicity and crime, but has chosen to list all the explanations she or he knows about this issue rather than focus in on the debate about the validity of official statistics in relation to ethnicity. Nevertheless, there is some discussion of the official statistics within the answer and the student demonstrates some good knowledge all the way through. The student therefore receives 7 marks for AO1 and 5 marks for AO2, 12 in total. This is a solid C-grade answer.

🅔 **Overall mark: 12/21**

A-grade answer

> The picture presented by the official statistics on crime and ethnic minorities would consist of a concentration of criminality among certain sections of ethnic young males **a**. This is known as disproportionate representation (Item B) **b**. It is particularly young black (Afro-Caribbean) males who are over-represented in the statistics of recorded crime and in the prison population and South Asians (Indians, Pakistanis and Bangladeshis) who are under-represented. In approaching ethnicity and criminality, it is vital to categorise different ethnic groups separately rather than using a catch-all category such as 'Black' to include very different cultures and traditions **c**, as is suggested by the third approach in Item B

🅔 This first paragraph sets out clearly the features of the official statistics to be discussed. **a b** Right from the start, the student has shown awareness of the danger of lumping all ethnic minorities together and draws upon the information in Item B to set the scene here. **c** A synoptic point about methodology, made at the end of the paragraph, sets the tone for the whole answer.

> Allowing for differences in crime rates between ethnic groups, there does seem to be a statistical correlation between Afro-Caribbean young males and a higher rate of crime. But even this seeming straightforward connection is subject to criticism **d**. For example, Morris (1976) points out that the official statistics that suggest this are based on the arrest rates of the police and not the actual amount of crime committed by different groups. When the evidence of self-report studies is taken into consideration, then the greater 'criminality' of young black men is less obvious, as roughly proportionate numbers of men from all backgrounds will report their crime. This suggests that the activities of the police in relation to young blacks need to be taken into consideration.

e **d** This paragraph contains good evaluation, made all the more powerful because it is supported with a reference to its source. The two approaches could be linked to the Item more specifically, but the answer has already done that in the preceding paragraph.

Another problem with taking the official statistics of crime and generalising to the population of ethnic minorities is the issue of multiple offending **e**. If for example there was in the statistics a high concentration of offences in localities with a high concentration of ethnic minorities, it might be that there are only a small number of individuals engaged in lots of criminal activity. To say from this that ethnic minorities are more 'criminal' is to make a generalisation that is not supportable.

e **e** Another telling criticism of taking the official statistics at face value is made in this paragraph. Marks are being gained for both the synoptic understanding shown and the complexity of the argument that is being built up.

There is thus a debate as to the real rate of criminal activity amongst the young ethnic population, especially Afro-Caribbeans. More sophisticated statistical analyses take into account many other factors when looking at ethnicity and crime. Stevens and Willis suggested that, even taking into account the activities of the police, there were higher levels of arrest for assault and robbery among Afro-Caribbeans, thus supporting the first position in the Item **f**. Other sociologists such as Cashmore argue that the reason young blacks appear more in the official statistics is because of hard policing of ethnic minority areas and institutional racism (Macpherson) among the police, which is more in line with the second position **g**.

e **f g** This is a balanced paragraph showing the dispute between two points of view in the Item over the interpretation of the official statistics. This direct comparison of opposing points of view is a good technique for showing your evaluation skills. The paragraph would have benefited from an explanation of the reference to the Macpherson Report rather than just the mention of the name.

The routine activities theory can be applied to the way that the police try to police the population. It has been shown that there are stereotypes of black men held by the police that are likely to lead to more blacks than whites being stopped and searched, and more arrests of blacks made. The irony is that these stereotypes of greater criminality are likely to be developed in part as a reaction to the official statistics that show more blacks commit crime. By acting as if this was true, the police may arrest disproportionate numbers of black criminals rather than white criminals, thus creating a self-fulfilling prophecy. This can operate the other way as well **h**, in that if South Asians are stereotyped as less criminal they are less likely to be targeted by the police and thus appear in the statistics. Other sociologists, however, suggest that it is the greater community controls over young South Asians that make it more difficult for them to get in trouble **i**.

e There is a great deal in this paragraph and all of it is worthy, even if it does cover many points. The tone of the paragraph is **h** evaluative and **i** synoptic, applying the theory of routine activities to the over- and under-representation issue. The reappearance of South Asians in this paragraph shows that the student has followed through on her or his points in the initial paragraph.

> To conclude, there is a problem with the statistics that show the relationship between ethnic minorities and crime. That problem is the issue of validity **j**. Do the official statistics show the real rate of criminal activity amongst ethnic minorities and therefore show a greater criminality among Afro-Caribbeans and a lesser criminality amongst South Asians? If they do, then it will help society and the forces of law and order to use their resources to combat crime in a more efficient way. If they don't, then it could be that the statistics are reinforcing institutional racism and unfairness to certain ethnic groups. From a sociological point of view the use of official statistics is also important because accepting them as valid or not will affect the types of explanations that the sociologist would look for. I do not think that the statistics tell the whole story of ethnicity and crime and therefore they should be treated with caution.

(e) This is a concluding paragraph of merit. **j** It applies the concept of validity well to attempt to come to a conclusion and at the end the student lays out what she or he thinks about the issue (evaluation). This is fine because the opinion is based on the evidence laid out in the body of the answer. However, the sociological support (studies and sociologists) is less well developed. A sophisticated understanding is being demonstrated here, but it is the AO2 skills that shine through. The answer merits a high mark because it keeps its focus on the issue of statistics and ethnicity, as required by the question. It thus gains 7 marks for AO1, but 12 for AO2, a total of 19. This answer would easily achieve an A grade.

(e) **Overall mark: 19/21**

Question 03 Applying your knowledge and understanding of sociological research methods

Read Item C and answer the question that follows.

Item C

The emergence of the 'mean girl' as a figure to be feared has been claimed to be one of the more negative unintended consequences of feminism. In this claim, the search for equivalence is said to have prompted a growth in female engagement in violence, especially through the appearance of the girl gang. Media images of young females attacking each other after heavy drinking sessions have fuelled a moral panic about the increasing incivility of young women and their willingness to engage in violence and in criminality. While it is not yet of the order of male involvement in such acts, its very existence seems to shock traditional sections of the public and raise doubts about the legitimacy of the feminist approach.

(03) Using material from Item C and elsewhere, evaluate the strengths and weaknesses of using participant observation to study girl gangs. (15 marks)

e Like all methods in context questions, you need to read the question very carefully to isolate what method you are required to write about and the issue or social group that you have to refer to. While it often seems obvious (the answer here would be participant observation and girl gangs respectively), it is important that you keep coming back to the specifics of the question when you are writing your answer. It is easy to start writing about other aspects, such as non-participant observation or girl criminals generally. You always need to make your points directly about what is being asked, so keep reminding yourself to do this.

C-grade answer

Participant observation (PO) is where a sociologist takes part in the activities of a group **a**. The main advantage of doing participant observation is that the sociologist can get a taste of the real-life experiences of the group under study, in this case girl gangs. If the sociologist just did a questionnaire **b** with girl gang members, she would not get the rich details of their lives but a superficial understanding of what it was like to be in a girl gang.

e This is a good start to the answer. **a** The student has offered a straightforward and accurate definition of participant observation and **b** showed evaluation skills by contrasting one of its advantages with another method. Although this is just the opening paragraph, it would have strengthened the answer if the references to girl gangs were more tied into the point.

Another advantage of doing participant observation is that the sociologist sees 'life in the raw', unclouded by the girl gang members' descriptions of what they say happened **c**. For example, if a girl gang member was describing a fight to the sociologist, then the sociologist is dependent on her words to make a judgement about how violent it was **d**. However, through participant observation, the sociologist is able to see the fight for herself and assess how violent it was. This is important, because girl gang members are supposed to be engaged in a 'search for equivalence' **e**, that is, be just as violent as boy gang members and the method of participant observation allows this to be checked independently.

e **c** Here is another advantage identified and explained well with a **d** good example. **e** Although the student slightly misuses the concept of a 'search for equivalence', the basic point made is a good one and highlights one of the advantages of personal observation.

However, there are several disadvantages in using participant observation and these would apply to a study of girl gangs. They are often described as the problems of 'getting in, staying in and getting out'. The main problem facing a sociologist who

wanted to study girl gangs would be the issue of access **f**. First, how would the sociologist make contact with a girl gang? Sociologists are often middle class and do not have ready access to worlds of violence, such as girl gangs. Even if the sociologist did make contact, she would then have to be accepted as a participating member of the girl gang. This means that she would have to be female, as it is unlikely that a male researcher would be accepted.

e **f** The important point about this paragraph is that the answer is making direct reference to a disadvantage associated with studying a girl gang. This is exactly what the better answers to question 03 should be doing — connecting evaluative points to the specific features of the aspects of crime and deviance asked about in the question.

Staying in and getting out **g** are mainly ethical problems. If the girl gang is engaged in illegal activity, the sociologist is placed in a difficult situation, as the sociologist shouldn't do anything that is illegal, but as a citizen they should report the actions to the police. When the research project is at an end, there are also ethical considerations to be made about whether the girl gangs have a right to review what is being said about them in the sociologist's report.

e **g** These disadvantages are less well connected to the issue of girl gangs, as they could be made about any participant observation study that involved illegal activity that comes to an end. It is not that these points do not score marks — they do — but they would be higher if the specific nature of girl gangs were kept to the fore.

In conclusion, the richness of the data collected by participant observation is offset by a number of practical problems in carrying out a participant observation study.

e Though a limited conclusion, it does try to sum up the points made in the main body of the answer. However, it is always worth mentioning the subject of the question (girl gangs) in the final paragraph and showing what specifically is good or difficult about the technique. This answer would attract 7 out of 15 marks.

e **Overall mark: 7/15**

A-grade answer

The nature and activities of girl gangs pose both specific and general advantages and disadvantages **a** for the sociologist who wants to use a participant observation technique. Participant observation is where the sociologist becomes a member of the group under study and carries out the same activities to give her or him insight into their social world. Participant observation can be either covert (hidden) or overt (some or all the gang members know they are being studied) **b**.

e This is a good opening paragraph, **a** setting out that the answer will deal with general and specific issues and **b** introducing a basic distinction between different types of participant observation.

This creates the first specific problem in using participant observation (PO) to study girl gangs. It would be impossible for a male researcher to do a covert PO study of girl gangs as he would be instantly recognisable as a non-member **c**. Therefore, a female researcher would have to be the choice and this raises theoretical issues. If the female researcher is a feminist, she may be sympathetic to the girls in the gang and be in danger of 'going native'. It is difficult for researchers to keep objective doing PO techniques and this might be a problem where a female researcher is studying female subjects only **d**.

e **c** This paragraph demonstrates a good understanding of the general disadvantages of PO, but applies that disadvantage specifically to the characteristics of girl gangs — that is, they are all female. **d** The point being made towards the end might be contentious, as it could imply that feminists are unable to be objective in looking at feminine phenomena, but it is quite a sophisticated point being put forward and should be rewarded.

Another problem with all PO studies is the issue of making contact with the people the sociologist wants to study and then gaining their acceptance. This is more difficult for any researcher into girl gangs, because they are more rare **e** than boy or mixed gangs and would therefore be more difficult to contact and approach **f**. On the other hand, once an initial contact was made, it might be that girl gangs would be more willing to participate, precisely because so little sociological research has been done on them and they would be 'first in the field' **g**. This might give the girl gang some status in the community, if it was known that a researcher was interested in them.

e **e** Again, this is a general problem related specifically to the nature of girl gangs and so scores highly on the skill of application. It also shows a **f** disadvantage and a possible **g** advantage around the issue of contact.

The fact that girl gangs are by definition female may also pose some theoretical difficulties for the researcher, as well as the practical ones. The stereotype of femininity, which is hegemonic in society, is one in which women are categorised as 'carers' and not given to violence in the main **h**. If the sociologist was to witness acts of violence committed by girl gang members, there is a danger that she might over-react to the situation because it transgresses our common-sense notions about women and violence **i**. The researcher must, therefore, be careful to be aware of her 'domain assumptions' **j** about women at all times and seek to be objective when analysing her data.

e This is another good paragraph, on two counts. **h** First, the student continues to take a general issue and show how it pertains to the **i** specific situation of girl gangs. **j** Second, it uses some good sociological concepts relevantly to support the point being made.

There are other disadvantages when doing participant observation, which would apply to all PO studies of gangs, whether male or female. There are ethical dilemmas for the sociologist in witnessing criminal activity, recording difficulties for the researcher in writing up her field notes, and the issue of informed consent to consider. These are issues that would also have to be considered in doing a PO study of girl gangs **k**.

ⓔ **k** Here the student is drawing our attention to the more general problems of PO, but makes the point that these would also apply to a PO study of girl gangs.

The advantages of using PO to study girl gangs are mainly concerned with the novel nature of such an endeavour **l**. Girl gangs are said to have emerged relatively recently and are therefore under-researched. It is an area of social life that has many innovative features and which dissolves a traditional male/female boundary. It is, therefore, of great interest to sociologists of gender as well as criminologists, because girl gangs seem to 'go against the grain' of our understandings of society **m**. What a PO study of a girl gang would be able to do is to explore the motivations and activities of members of girl gangs in great depth. Through interacting with girl gang members, the sociologist would build up a rich picture of why the girls become gang members, their social backgrounds, and the emotional and social satisfactions that they experience in being part of a gang. More importantly, by participating in the activities themselves, the sociologist can 'stand in the shoes' of the girl gang member and experience exactly what they are experiencing. This insight into a previously hidden world would be a real advantage of PO.

ⓔ **l** The answer has moved onto the advantages of PO and though these are of a general nature, **m** the student is careful to keep the focus of girl gangs throughout the paragraph.

In conclusion, there are some specific problems associated with a PO study of girl gangs. The major problem seems to be gaining acceptance within a girl gang, so that the study can be carried out as impartially as possible. However, these difficulties are, in my opinion, outweighed **n** by the insights that sociologists can gain about an 'alien' social world and so illuminate a new development in crime and deviance.

ⓔ **n** This is a well-balanced conclusion, but with the student definitely coming down on one side and therefore showing evaluation skills. The answer overall is not totally comprehensive — there are other advantages and disadvantages that might have been used. Only 15 marks are available and what the student does really well is focus on the specific issue of girl gangs. Hence, it would score 14 out of 15.

ⓔ **Overall mark: 14/15**

Example 2

Question 01 Labelling theory and crime

Read Item A and answer the question that follows.

Item A

Traditional approaches to crime and deviance focus on the character of the deviant or the social circumstances of the deviant's upbringing, where he or she lives or how poor the deviant is. Other approaches shift attention towards what happens after a criminal act has been committed. They involve the agents of law and order in the active creation of the phenomenon we call crime through the process of labelling. They also point to the power of the media in creating images of what it means to be deviant in society.

(01) Using material from Item A and elsewhere, evaluate the advantages and disadvantages of labelling theory in understanding crime and deviance. (21 marks)

ⓔ The focus of this question is on a specific approach to the study of crime and deviance, that is, labelling theory. However, you can choose to consider its weaknesses by looking at how other approaches might be critical of it. You need to provide a balance of advantages and disadvantages of the approach, making sure that you come to a reasonable conclusion about the balance of advantages and disadvantages that emerges from the points you have made in your answer.

C-grade answer

Labelling theory has been criticised and supported in a number of different ways. Interactionists wish to get to the real processes behind crime and deviance. They argue that labelling by social agencies such as the police is much more important in understanding crime than any other factor **a**. Positivists argue that it is based on a wrong methodology **b**. Structuralists argue that labelling theorists ignore important social factors, which might cause crime and deviance, such as poverty, inequality and the like and also ignore the original deviant act as if it was not real **c**.

ⓔ There are some theoretical elements here in referring to the **a** interactionist, **b** positivist and **c** structuralist approaches. These theoretical criticisms are acceptable, but they could do with some exemplification to show the examiner that the student really understands what is meant by these approaches. **b c** The comments on these approaches include evaluation.

There is a difference between primary deviation and secondary deviation (Lemert) **d**. Primary deviation is the initial deviant action, such as breaking a window

AQA A2 Sociology

or truanting from school. This is the sort of thing that everybody does at some time or another and it is not particularly remarkable **e**. If you get caught when you do these things, you then can become a secondary deviant, because everybody knows you have done something wrong and they begin to act towards you as a vandal or a skiver from school. This might mean that your parents won't let you out at night because you might get into trouble again, or the teacher always assumes that you are 'wagging it' when you are really ill **f**.

(e)   **d** The student is describing a basic idea behind labelling. **e** While it is not always expressed in sociological language, the student is demonstrating that she or he has a good basic knowledge of the processes. **f** There is also a synoptic dimension to this paragraph in the example of truanting from school, although this could be made more explicit.

The many advantages of labelling come from the way that interactionists look at how the police, the courts and the media attach labels to some individuals and not to others who have carried out the same actions **g**. This shows that crime and deviance is socially constructed **h** and is not 'obvious' when it happens. By focusing attention on what happens after the initial criminal act, labelling allows sociologists to gain a fuller understanding **i** of crime and deviance as a social activity and not just something done by 'law-breakers'.

(e)   **g** The advantages of labelling are developed further in this paragraph and the student is correct to draw attention to the role of social agencies in the process of differential labelling. **h** The student makes good use of sociological concepts in this paragraph, but needs to develop the ideas that are being established. **i** It would be helpful to write more about what is meant by a 'fuller' understanding, to make clear the contribution of labelling theory.

There are different types of interactionists that use labelling theory **j** to emphasise different aspects of crime and deviance. For example, phenomenologists show that, because of processes such as labelling, the official statistics of crime do not represent the real level of criminal activity in society. There are many criminal actions that are undiscovered and therefore not labelled or are ignored by the police because they may not have enough evidence to label someone as a criminal **k**.

(e)   **j** This is a fair attempt to point out that there is more than one approach to labelling theory, but the answer does not offer a very sophisticated view of what is involved in the labelling process. **k** While it is true that the police might not count an action because they do not have enough evidence to proceed, there are other reasons why a criminal act might never be labelled as such. A more detailed account would help the student to show a more sophisticated understanding of the advantages of these approaches.

Labelling theorists argue that your gender, class and ethnic origin are important in determining whether you are processed as a deviant or not by the police (secondary deviance). But it might just be that being known to the police or having a criminal record anyway might be more important. A more controversial view of labelling is

that it treats those labelled as passive victims of the process with no say in it at all. This is odd for a theory that is supposed to be interactionist **l**.

e There are a couple of criticisms in this paragraph, **l** with the last one being quite sophisticated. However, there is not enough detail given in the paragraph to make it clear what the disadvantage is.

Therefore, there are a number of disadvantages and advantages to the labelling approach to crime and deviance. The main advantage is the way that labelling theories draw attention to the activities of law enforcement officers **m** and the main disadvantage is that it suggests that those being labelled cannot resist being labelled as deviant or criminal. **n** However, it can be concluded that labelling does offer a different way of looking at crime and deviance from other sociological viewpoints and is therefore important.

e This is the concluding paragraph and **m** the student does try to summarise the main advantage and **n** disadvantage of the approach and then tries to come to a conclusion about how useful it is. Although the points made are valid (indeed, the point about resistance could have been more developed) they would need to be more sophisticated to score more highly. The answer would be awarded 11 out of 21 marks.

e **Overall mark: 11/21**

A-grade answer

Labelling theory was developed initially by Becker to explore the ways that the social control agencies created deviants and criminals through their everyday activities **a**. It was in opposition to the approach that saw the deviant population as somehow different to the mainstream population, and who could therefore be easily recognised and 'dealt with'. Becker argued that it was not any specific action that was inherently deviant, nor any particular group who were deviant. Rather, it was the activities of the police and courts (and the media some would argue) that attached the label of deviant to individuals and groups **b**. Others, carrying out exactly the same activities, would not be labelled as deviant.

e **a** This is a good basic introduction to the work of Becker, which it is necessary to establish before the criticisms can be discussed. **b** There is enough here to make it clear that the student has a good understanding of the difference in approach between traditional explanations and Becker's views.

The advantage of labelling over traditional ways of trying to control deviants and criminals is that labelling theorists argue that we all commit deviant and criminal acts **c**. It is however, only some of us who are then labelled as criminals. This is more true to real life, as we know that we have all broken the law — for example by speeding in a car **d**. By looking at how social control agencies operate, interactionists are able to show that crime is not obvious or natural, but rather it is a product of social processes, that is, it is socially constructed **e**. The importance of this is that it is less important what an individual does, but more important about how the social control agencies react to the individual's action **f**.

e **c** The answer gets straight to an important advantage of the approach, that it does not follow the usual lines of enquiry in approaching crime and deviance. **d** It supports the idea that this different approach gives us a new way of looking at crime with an example to support the point being made. **e** The student uses a sociological concept to show their understanding of this important difference, **f** but develops the concept to illustrate why it is an advantage.

The interesting question that labelling theory asks is, 'If we all commit crime, why are only some groups and individuals singled out to be labelled as criminals?' They then turn to the routine activities of the courts, the police and the media to examine why some are stigmatised by labels and others are not. For example, where the police choose to patrol will affect who gets caught and labelled and who does not and the police tend to patrol more in areas associated with poverty and disadvantage **g**. However, it is more complicated than just being caught by the police. The police may choose to issue a warning rather than arrest someone. Interactionists suggest that stereotypes held by the police and social control agents come into play when these decisions are made. So, if you are black, young, working class and male, you are more likely to get caught up in labelling processes than if you are white and middle class **h**.

e This paragraph begins to build up a detailed account of why some groups and individuals get labelled and others do not. **g** It is not a comprehensive account of these processes, but picks out one or two aspects that are illustrative of labelling. In the time available to answer the question, this is a good decision. **h** The point being made is clearly expressed through the use of a question and then the point is related to the social distribution of crime that appears in the official statistics.

However, critics of the labelling approach argue that the application of a label is assumed rather than empirically shown. For example, it is not clear how often a label has to be applied before it sticks. 'Does it have to be an official such as a police officer or a teacher who applies the label before the process kicks in?' critics ask **i**. There is also the problem that the idea of a master status suggests that the label becomes the most dominant form of identity by the labelled **j**. Those who oppose labelling suggest that there are many contradictory sources of identity **k** available to individuals and it is unlikely that one of them becomes so dominant that it blocks out all others.

e **i j** There are two lines of critique here, both expressed at a level of sophistication that will attract reward. The student is applying some good concepts, **k** such as identity, which is part of one of the themes of the A-level specification. This will gain marks. The student is also using concepts from within labelling — such as 'master status' — to good effect.

Last l, the idea of a self-fulfilling prophecy has also come under attack. The argument is that acting in accordance with a label is just one of several outcomes that might come about m. An equally likely reaction by an individual to being labelled 'thick' is to try and show the teacher who has done the labelling that he or she is wrong. This is known as the self-negating prophecy. Another reaction might be to ignore the label completely, because it is unimportant to the individual so labelled. This might be harder to do if it is the criminal justice system that is doing the labelling, as conviction as a criminal is a very public label to be landed with.

e l This is signalled as the last criticism. m Again, there is a level of sophisticated understanding shown here about the complexities of the labelling process and how it is not an automatic or deterministic process.

So, while labelling theory can be attractive to sociologists in looking at different areas of social life, it is not without its problems. It does help us to understand that there is much to be learned by looking at the activities of law enforcers n, as well as the actions of those who are labelled as criminal, but we need to be careful that we do not reduce individuals to just their labels o.

e Although this looks like a short conclusion, it is fair enough in the time that the student has available. Perhaps the last point about reducing individuals to their label could have been explained more clearly, but the student has hit upon a major n advantage and o disadvantage in this conclusion. As the student clearly has a sophisticated understanding of these, this answer would gain 19 out of 21 marks.

e **Overall mark: 19/21**

Question 02 **Self-report and victim studies**

Read Item B and answer the question that follows.

Item B

The official statistics of crime do not count all the crimes that are committed in a society, but rather, they represent a proportion of criminal activity. There are many reasons why a criminal act might not appear in the official statistics, but once sociologists recognised this 'absence' they looked to ways of researching into crime that might try to uncover what had previously been hidden. Self-report studies and victim surveys are two of the ways in which they explored the 'real' extent of crime.

> **(02) Using material from Item B and elsewhere, assess the usefulness of self-report studies and victimisation studies to establish the extent of crime.**
>
> (21 marks)

e As always, you are required to make reference to the Item where appropriate. The key point to note about this question is that you should try to provide a balance between material on self-report studies and on victimisation studies. In assessing the usefulness of these two instruments, it would help you to score high marks if you could differentiate between them in their relative advantages and disadvantages. In coming to a conclusion, you should consider whether one of them is more useful than the other, and if so, why.

C-grade answer

Self-report studies are where respondents 'shop' themselves, by owning up to crimes they have committed **a**. Victimisation studies are where the individual is asked to report when they have been a victim of a crime, even if they have not reported it to the police **b**. These are two ways in which sociologists have tried to find out about crime **c**.

e **a b** The answer begins with definitions of the two research instruments that are being asked about — self-report studies and victimisation studies. **c** The student attempts to show what these are in relation to the study of crime, but could have extended this part of the answer, for example by writing about how they are related to the extent of crime and the patterns of crime in society.

The uses of self-report studies are that they can discover crimes that are not recorded in the official statistics **d**. Many criminal acts are not detected by the police or do not appear in court records because they are not proceeded with by the law enforcement agencies. This means that there is crime that does not appear anywhere in the official accounts of crime **e**. The idea behind self-report studies is that if you ask people about their own criminal activity, you will uncover more crime than is usually seen in the official statistics. Of course, respondents to self-report studies must be confident that they will be anonymous in any sociological work that uses them **f**.

e **d** The main advantage of self-report studies is shown here and there is a solid understanding of why they are used. **e** The reasons for the non-appearance of criminal acts in the statistics could have been elaborated further by the student — there are many reasons why crime does not get recorded as such. **f** The paragraph also draws attention to a necessary pre-condition for the success of self-report studies.

One of the problems with this is that it is not always clear that the respondent is telling the truth, as they may lie to the researcher **g**.

e **g** This leads on to a disadvantage of self-report studies. However, the student does not explain the problem fully enough and relies on a tautology for some of the explanation ('not telling the truth' and 'lying' are nearly the same thing). If the student was making a subtle distinction between these two (not being fully honest and bare-faced lying), then it is not explained well. It

could be that the respondent is mis-remembering, exaggerating or downplaying events, or that he or she has decided not to reveal what might be seen as a serious crime.

A second problem with using self-report studies is the issue of sampling. How does the researcher know that they have a representative sample of the population to do their research? It might be that they are not representative in some way **h**.

ⓔ **h** This is an instructive paragraph, as the point made is a general one that could be made about any survey, not just self-report studies. It does score marks, but it would have been better if the student could have related it much more firmly to self-report studies in the explanation.

Last, self-report studies that rely on interviews rather than postal questionnaires **i**, may suffer from 'interviewer effect'. Interviewees may be more reluctant to confess to crimes face-to-face than through the anonymity of a questionnaire. Guarantees of confidentiality may not be convincing to some respondents.

ⓔ **i** This paragraph does score marks because the student has made the point directly relevant to the issue of self-reporting. By bringing in the setting for the collection of the research, the student is able to explain the point carefully.

Victimisation studies are a second way in which sociologists have tried to investigate crime beyond the official statistics. They are often seen as more reliable and valid **j** than self-report studies because people are more likely to reveal that they have been a victim of crime than that they have committed a crime **k**.

ⓔ **k** The student turns to the second half of the question and does this well by relating an advantage that victimisation studies have over self-report studies. **j** The student also uses correct sociological concepts in relation to this advantage.

Though victimisation studies might be more valid, they do have their problems as well. It is difficult to know whether a crime has actually been committed or whether the respondent just thinks that they have suffered from a criminal act **l**. Most respondents would not be familiar with the law in enough detail **m**. The sociologist would then have to make a decision as to whether the respondent had really been a victim or just thought that they were **n**.

ⓔ **l** There is a good point being made about the disadvantages of victimisation surveys, but it is not always clearly expressed. **m** An example of where knowledge of the law would be useful to respondents would help here. **n** The idea that the sociologist still has to make a decision about the victim's report could have been expanded to show a more sophisticated understanding. Overall, the answer is a solid response, identifying some advantages and disadvantages in a balanced way. The points made are varied in their quality, but the student does show sociological skills in answering this question. This answer would attract 10 out of 21 marks.

ⓔ **Overall mark: 10/21**

A-grade answer

Self-report studies, such as the British Crime Survey, use a combination of interviews and questionnaire items to establish what crimes individuals say they have committed over the previous year **a**. Victimisation studies are also used by official bodies as ways of getting a fuller picture of the extent **b** and distribution **c** of crimes, and involve asking a representative sample of the public which crimes they perceive they have been a victim of over the preceding period **d**.

e   **a d** These are very good definitions of both instruments and the student shows some knowledge of the main self-report study, the BCS. **b c** The student packs in some important words into this paragraph that illustrate a deep understanding of what these things are.

The use of self-report and victim studies by sociologists and statisticians has come about because of dissatisfaction with the official records of the extent of crime **e**. The official statistics do not include many actions that people see as criminal activity, with the result that there is a 'dark figure' **f** of crime. The dark figure refers to all those crimes that never appear in the official statistics but which might be uncovered by the use of these two instruments.

e   **e** The student has chosen to begin the discussion of the advantages of both instruments together and this is a good tactic. The answer carefully relates the shortcomings of the official statistics with the effects of the two types of survey. **f** In addition, the student uses the correct sociological concept in this context and explains what it actually means.

The idea behind these approaches is that, by asking people to either reveal their own criminal activities or to recount what crimes they have been a victim of, the sociologist will find a more valid, fuller picture of crime in society **g**. For example, it might be that middle-class crime such as 'fiddling expenses', might hardly ever appear in the officials statistics, because the police are not that concerned with it, but it might show up in self-report studies, as long as people were confident they would not get into trouble by 'confessing' **h**. Some criminal acts might not get reported to the police because they were seen as too trivial or because the victim was not sure they had been conned or cheated, but respondents might be prepared to put these down in a victim survey. In these instances, the instruments reveal more about the extent and the patterns of crime, with victimisation surveys revealing more than self-report studies **i**.

e   This is a very effective paragraph for two main reasons. **g** First, the answer brings together some of the advantages of both self-report and victimisation surveys. **h** It supports the points being made with appropriate examples and distinguishes between the two types of survey in doing so. **i** Second, in a sophisticated ending, the student indicates that there are also some other differences between the two types of survey that can be linked to disadvantages.

The first problem with both self-report and victimisation surveys, therefore, is with their validity **j**. The sociologist has no way of knowing how truthful respondents are being **k**. They may exaggerate their involvement to show off (it has been shown that boys are more prone to do this than girls) or not report criminal actions of which they are particularly ashamed (the reverse is the case here) **l**. There are also ethnic differences in the willingness of participants to report their criminality. Victims are more likely to be truthful than those who have committed undetected crimes **m**.

e This is a good paragraph for a number of reasons. **j** First, it uses sociological concepts to establish the point. **k** Second, it clearly sets out what the problem is and **l** then goes on to explain it through the use of examples. **l** The student is also aware of the dual nature of the problem; that is, they can lead to under- or over-reporting of crime. **m** Again, the student is careful to show that there is a difference between the two types of reporting.

A second problem with self-report studies is the strategy adopted to allow self-reporting to take place. The respondent is presented with a number of criminal scenarios and then asked to indicate if she or he has done the action in the previous year. The purpose of this strategy is to act as a prompt to the memory, as a question that simply asked 'what crimes did you commit last year?' assumes the respondent will know if she or he has committed a crime and report them all **n**. However, the list of crimes is problematic. It represents what the researcher thinks are important crimes and may omit crimes that the respondents have committed, and therefore paint a false picture of the extent of crime **o**. For example, items about cybercrimes may not be included in the questionnaire.

e This is another good paragraph. **n** It goes off the point a little in the middle when writing about a question it does not contain, **o** but brings it back firmly to the question at the end. Victim studies are not included in this paragraph, but that is fine as the student is making a point specifically about self-report studies.

Last, there are ethical and moral issues **p** to do with self-report and victimisation studies. Although the researcher promises confidentiality, what should the researcher do if a respondent self-reported a really bad crime, such as a murder or a big robbery? **q** Or a victim declared a crime of physical or mental abuse? **r** This would create a moral dilemma for the sociologist and place her or him in an impossible situation.

e **p** The last point is an interesting one. It is a hypothetical case, but it is relevant and related specifically to the issue of **q** self-reporting and to **r** victim studies. Overall, this is an excellent answer. It is not perfect, in that the balance between the two types of instrument is slightly skewed towards self-report studies, but it still gains 20 out of 21 marks.

e **Overall mark: 20/21**

Question 03 **Applying research methods to an issue in crime and deviance**

Here is another Methods in Context question for you to attempt yourself.

Read Item C and answer the following question.

Item C

Increasingly, sociological attention is moving away from petty crime and small-time criminals to look at the criminal activities of the powerful. The sociological gaze has fallen on a number of different powerful formations. One area of interest is organised crime and the way that such activities have become international. Another is called corporate crime and is about members of big companies committing crimes in the pursuit of their corporate objectives. More recently, sociological interest has grown in international terrorism and how it operates in a globalised world. Last, the activities of the state itself have come under scrutiny, from violations of human rights to genocide.

(03) Using information from Item C and elsewhere, assess the advantages and disadvantages of using EITHER secondary documents OR unstructured interviews to investigate 'crimes of the powerful'.

(15 marks)

e   The difference in this Methods in Context question is that you have a choice of method to make and, once made, you must keep to it and not stray into writing about the other one. Note also that crimes of the powerful might incorporate several different forms of criminal behaviour — as long as you stick with the definition you present yourself, you will be answering the question.

Knowledge check answers

1 Differential association.
2 Target-hardening.
3 Self-fulfilling prophecy.
4 Examples might include: the working class, ethnic minorities, women, the disabled, gay people.
5 The square of crime.
6 A concept developed by Murray to describe those at the bottom of society who are characterised by family breakdown, welfare dependency and unemployment.
7 Discourses are a series of statements or events that define relationships between elements of the social world and shape what we do and what we do not do.
8 Self-report studies and victimisation studies.
9 Social workers, traffic wardens, council officials.
10 A masculine attitude that emphasises pride, strength and dominance over women.
11 Corporate crime is carried out to the benefit of the business organisation and usually increases profits; white-collar crime is committed against the business organisation and usually results in a financial loss.
12 Saying to yourself that 'nobody got hurt' or 'it's nobody else's business' or 'they were asking for it' etc.
13 The process whereby manufacturing and extractive industries decline, so that fewer citizens work in manual occupations.

14 The most frequently cited are prostitution and infanticide.
15 Social capital is where there are strong family and community networks which support individuals and which individuals can draw on in times of need.
16 A representation of social reality that suggests there are many variations along a line between two opposite phenomena.
17 There are many possible groups, from the classic mods and rockers to the more recent looters on the streets of cities.
18 Global warming or the extinction of species are both examples.
19 The United Nations.
20 The police act against all forms of crime, whether trivial or significant, with the idea that always acting against seemingly minor forms of criminal behaviour will lead to falls in all types of crime.
21 The bourgeoisie.
22 Closed circuit television.
23 There are a large number of these from dead locks on doors to cans of gas to ever larger bicycle chains.
24 Not eating and starving to death is one example.
25 Because they exist mainly in areas where there is economic insecurity and a need for short-term loans to tide people over hard times.
26 Police, forensic scientists, morticians, coroners etc.
27 Through any suicide note that may be left.

Page numbers in **bold** refer to **key term definitions**

AQA A2 Sociology